LOOK EAST POLICY
IMPACT ON NORTHEAST INDIA

LOOK EAST POLICY
Impact on Northeast India

Edited by

Charles Reuben Lyngdoh
Merostar Rani

SYNOD COLLEGE
SHILLONG-793002 (INDIA)

AKANSHA PUBLISHING HOUSE
NEW DELHI-110002 (INDIA)

AKANSHA PUBLISHING HOUSE
4649/21-B, Ansari Road
Daryaganj, New Delhi - 110 002
Phones: 23263193, 9811582579
E-mail: ektabooks@yahoo.com

Look East Policy: Impact on Northeast India

First Published, 2008

ISBN 978-81-8370-124-2

The views expressed in the articles are the personal opinions of the contributors. Neither Synod College nor the Editors nor the Publisher take responsibility for them, whatsover.

PRINTED IN INDIA

Published by Akansha Publishing House, New Delhi and Synod College, Shillong and printed at Aryan Enterprise, Delhi.

CONTENTS

PREFACE

Development has been the foremost cry of the Northeast. In this decades' old quest the region has had to confront inevitable surging impressions ranging from the demands for statehood, political autonomy and political independence to global inevitabilities such as liberalization, privatization and globalization. These impressions have given rise to emerging individualism and consumerism while calling upon the region abundant in resources, to keep up with these changing strides. Development comes at a price, balancing the needs of the economy with ability of nature to absorb and sustain such needs.

The Look East Policy is one such proposal initiated by the central government to address Northeast's long standing covet for development. Introduced in the early nineties this policy was intended to direct a major portion of the Northeast's economic and commercial activities towards it eastern international neighbors. This proposal appears geographically viable for all the eight states of the region are cradled amidst five international neighbors — Nepal, Bhutan, the Tibet autonomous region of China, Myanmar and Bangladesh. It is intended that the inauguration of this policy will bring the Northeast tremendous possibility of engagement in various sectors with both the thriving as well as the emerging economies of South and Southeast Asia.

Keeping this objective in focus Synod College invited policy makers, public representatives, administrators, academicians, journalists, professionals and students to a two day national seminar on "Look East Policy: Impact on Northeast India' on October 19-20, 2006. This volume is the outcome of this seminar, a collection of speeches and papers that were discussed and deliberated upon.

There are a host of people and organizations who have been directly and indirectly involved in the preparation of this book. We would like to put on record our deep appreciation for all the assistance and encouragement that they have rendered. All praise and honor be to the Almighty who has been our guide and our inspiration each step of the way and who makes all things possible. We thank our Principal and our Vice Principal, the driving forces of this publication and for all the encouragement that they provide, the members of the Synod College Internal Quality Assurance Cell (IQAC) who continuously strive to enhance the academic environment of the College and the staff and students who have unfailingly supported all the endeavors of the College. A special thank you to our colleagues P.G. Marbaniang and A.K. Lyngdoh for all the assistance they have rendered. We are indeed grateful and appreciate the efforts of all the contributors who have taken the time to prepare papers on various themes associated with this topic. We also express our appreciation to the North Eastern Council for extending financial assistance towards organizing the seminar and for its continued faith and encouragement to all our programmes. A big thank you to our families who have been seeing less and less of us over the last few months and silently understand our commitments to the preparation of this book.

In ending we express our appreciation to Mr. M.P. Misra of Akansha Publishing House, New Delhi for having taken utmost care and responsibility to publish this book in record time.

Charles Reuben Lyngdoh
Merostar Rani

CONTRIBUTORS

Amiya Sarma, Lecturer, Department of Economics, Jagiroad College, Jagiroad, Assam.
amiyasarma1@yahoo.co.in

B.P. Muktieh, General Manager, Industrial Development Bank of India Ltd., North-Eastern Zonal Office, Guwahati, Assam.
bp.muktieh@idbi.co.in

Bhupen Kumar Sarma, Senior Lecturer, Department of Economics, Jagiroad College, Jagiroad, Assam.

Charles Reuben Lyngdoh, Head, Department of Political Science, Synod College, Shillong, Meghalaya.
reubenlyngdoh@yahoo.co.in

Daisy Das, Lecturer, Department of Economics, North Gauhati College, Guwahati, Assam.
daisy_iitg@yahoo.co.in

D.P. Tripathi, National General Secretary, Nationalist Congress Party, New Delhi.

I. Wanswett, Lecturer, Department of Economics, Synod College, Shillong, Meghalaya.
iwanswett@hotmail.com

Lambodar Rout, Lecturer, Department of Economics, Nongtalang College, Jaintia Hills, Meghalaya.

Merostar Rani, Coordinator, Internal Quality Assurance Cell, Synod College, Shillong, Meghalaya.
merostar_rani@yahoo.co.in

Mousumi Borah, Senior Lecturer, Department of Economics, Arya Vidyapeeth College, Guwahati, Assam.
mousumi_borah@sify.com

Purno A. Sangma, Member of Parliament (Lok Sabha), former Speaker (Lok Sabha), New Delhi.

Rajiv Pratap Rudy, former Union Minister of State, Commerce and Civil Aviation (Independent Charge), New Delhi.
rudy@rediffmail.com

Ratul Mahanta, Lecturer, Department of Economics, Gauhati University, Guwahati, Assam.
mahanta_r@yahoo.com

Sangita Kakoty, Senior Lecturer, Department of History, Arya Vidyapeeth College, Guwahati, Assam.
sangitakakoty@yahoo.co.in

LIST OF TABLES

WELCOME ADDRESS

—D. Wanswett

"Great things are not done by impulse but by a series of small things brought together".

With immeasurable pleasure I stand before you as the head of this institution to extend a hearty welcome to each and everyone who are expectantly gathered at the inauguration of this two-day National Seminar on "Look East Policy: Impact on Northeast India" and to express my heartfelt thanks to you for this encouraging response to our invitation. Words fail to express my gratitude to the Hon'ble Union Minister of State for Commerce, Shri Jairam Ramesh, who has come all the way from New Delhi not just to inaugurate the seminar and to deliver the keynote address but in the process share his precious thoughts and proficient views with us. Sir, we are greatly privileged and deeply inspired by your presence. Shri Jairam Ramesh has shown his concern and interest for the region by successively visiting four States of the Northeast — Assam, Mizoram, Manipur and now Meghalaya between June and October 2006.

We are indebted to the Hon'ble Chief Minister of Meghalaya, Shri J.D. Rymbai, who is also the President of the Synod College Alumni Association for his close association and guiding inspiration to our College. Sir, your presence in our midst is indeed very encouraging. I also extend a warm welcome to Dr. Donkupar Roy, the Deputy Chief Minister of

Meghalaya, Shri R.G. Lyngdoh, the Home Minister, Government of Meghalaya and Dr. D.D. Lapang, the Chairman, Meghalaya Economic Development Council. Shri Purno A. Sangma, Hon'ble Member of Parliament, and former Speaker of the Lok Sabha, our friend, philosopher and guide who has been a driving force to our noble mission and who has encouraged us to scale new heights. There is much that we owe to him in our growth and development as an educational institution of repute. I warmly welcome you, Sir, as I warmly welcome Shri Rajiv Pratap Rudy, former Union Minister of State, Commerce and Civil Aviation (Independent Charge) for his kind-heartedness and spontaneity in accepting our humble invitation to come to Shillong and to be a vital part of this discussion. We expectantly look forward to your highly esteemed views, Sir. At this time I also extend a warm welcome to the National General Secretary of the Nationalist Congress Party, Professor D. P. Tripathi, members of this seminar's Advisory Committee, senior officers of the Government of Meghalaya, members of the Synod College Governing Body, resource persons, invitees, participants and all present.

We are indeed humbled and proud that seldom a galaxy of such eminent persons has converged in Shillong under one roof to participate and to deliberate on a significantly current theme as the Look East Policy and its implications for the Northeast region. In planning the seminar we realized how important it was that this policy be given due focus that it deserves and looked at from new perspectives so that it would acquire new dimensions in the present world where evolution is the key word. The Government of India formulated this policy to explore new possibilities of interacting with its eastern neighbors at various levels thereby reducing its dependency on the West which had all along curtailed India's influence in world affairs. To this end the policy implies a new shift in focus. In place of the old tendency of the looking west India would now turn towards its eastern neighbors the vibrant economies of the Southeast Asia countries as new potential partners in international trade. The Southeast Asia countries and India are no strangers to one another. Their civilization links stretch thousands of years evident in culture, tradition, heritage, monuments, religion and linguistic influences. India's relationship with its Southeast Asia neighbors has been shaped by the events of time and the changing course of world politics. Today the time is ripe for India to put behind the cold war divisions of Asia and to set the tone for weaving a regional economic fabric with these countries on the lines of an "Asian Union". The Look East Policy is a work in progress, a policy that is continuously evolving. Its economic potential should be the most compelling factor to shift from rhetoric to a realistic approach especially when the momentum and pace of reforms have been set in the Indian economy. Today new security issues of a non-military nature have emerged and need to be addressed in a comprehensive manner. A pro-active approach to our eastern neighbors requires a clear vision for cementing better relationships.

Due to its proximity the northeastern part of India could turn to the South Asian and Southeast Asian countries to harness the benefits of economic development and reduce its over dependence on the centre while at the same time firmly remaining an integral part of the Indian constitutional and political framework. Undoubtedly, the implementation of the Look East Policy will have wide-ranging implications for the Northeast. From a vantage point of view the region is India's gateway to the East. It has been appropriately pointed out that the Look East Policy "envisages the northeast region not as the periphery of India, but as the centre of a thriving and integrated economic space linking two dynamic regions with a network of highways, railways, pipelines, transmission lines crisscrossing the region".

The eight states fall within a part of the country which shares 98% of its borders with its South Asian and Southeast Asian neighbors, hence, the unique strategic geo-political importance of this region to the rest of the country. Home to about 250 tribes with 190 spoken languages, it presents a rich tapestry of diverse and unique cultures and ethnic identities. The majority of its vast resources are yet untapped due to lack of basic infrastructure such as road and rail transport, communication network and financial institutions. The region is also known for its oldest democratic systems whose strength are in its indigenous institutions. It would be interesting to deliberate on the extent to which these may be impacted by the implementation of the Look East Policy. It is also a known fact that the region is presently grappling with problems of insurgency and general unrest. Growing population, urbanization and influx have all led to great unemployment problems. The Look East Policy has therefore become an area for animated discussion in debates and seminars such as this. It is in this regard that Synod College, Shillong is organizing the two day National Seminar on "Look East Policy – Impact on Northeast India" to deliberate on key areas associated with the theme.

Mark Twain once said, "*Take your mind out every now and then and dance on it*". That was his way of saying, "Try something new, break new ground". This is a good advice for all of us. Sometimes we need something to jolt us out of a lifeless routine – a bold new thought, a different slant on a familiar subject, or a bit of wisdom from someone who has walked down that road before we have.

There are high expectations from this Seminar, and we promise that nobody will be disappointed but all will be well benefited. I wish everybody prolific and constructive interactions.

Thank You.

KEYNOTE ADDRESS

Jairam Ramesh

The Principal of Synod College, Dr. D. Wanswett, Shri J.D. Rymbai, the Chief Minister of Meghalaya, other political leaders and dignitaries on the dias, Mr. P.A. Sangma, Dr. D.D. Lapang, Mr. R.G. Lyngdoh, Mr. Rajiv Pratap Rudy, Professor D.P. Tripathi, Ladies and Gentlemen

In the meeting held on October 18, 2006 with the Trade and Commerce Ministers of the eight member states of the North Eastern Council many issues were discussed on trade and infrastructure creation in the Northeast. The topic 'Look East Policy – Impact on Northeast India' has engaged the attention of many people in the Northeast. In fact there is more for "look east" in the Northeast than in the rest of India. This topic has also generated immense interest and enthusiasm and numerous queries have been posed by the young men and women of this region on the Look East Policy. I hope that this enthusiasm is also shared by the rest of India. What India needs is *look Northeast before looking east*. The Northeast is a region comprising of eight states most of which are wrought by problems of militancy and insurgency. When you have peace you do not have the headlines, it is only when you have ethnic violence, insurgency or militancy that you attract the national headlines. It is then that cabinet committees meet and special economic packages are formulated. Unfortunately there is a disadvantage of being peaceful. If you are violent the entire country imagines that you are up in flames and therefore the need to come up with some kind of development package or the other. Nevertheless, this topic has engaged the attention of many.

It has been the endeavor of successive governments to put in place a Look East Policy. Of course the Look East Policy is nothing new. We have always had a vision of India in a close relationship with the rest of Asia. Before India became independent, the first Asian Relations Conference chaired by Pandit Jawaharlal Nehru was held in 1946. This Conference drew leaders from all over Asia. We are not doing something new by advocating this policy. For many years though we propounded the Look East Policy but we went west. It's only in the last ten years that we are not only saying *look east* but also *go east*. The result of it is that this year Asia is now our largest trading partner. It is not the United States it is not Europe but it is Asia that is India's largest trading partner. This is not a coincidence but a cumulative effect of a set of actions that have been taken over the last ten to fifteen years to increase trade ties between India and the countries of the rest of Asia particularly the ASEAN countries, Japan and those of Northeast Asia. As a result of this increase in trade links and our engagement and investments, Indian companies are now making investments in the rest of the Asian region and Asian countries are also coming to India. This two ways street has been opened up and today Asia occupies a place of pride as far as trade is concerned. India is in the final stages of negotiating a free trade agreement with ASEAN which hopefully will be clinched, negotiated and finalized by the end of the year and this would be a major step forward. India already has a comprehensive economic partnership agreement with Singapore, and has the beginnings of a free trade agreement or rather a framework free trade agreement with Thailand. A free trade agreement with the ten countries of ASEAN to be finalized by the end of the year would hopefully constitute a significant milestone in India's Look East Policy. In addition, India is planning a large number of infrastructure projects in order to give political, economic and strategic content to its Look East Policy. Critical in this investment is the intensified engagement with Myanmar, a country with whom a State like Mizoram shares almost 1600 kms of its border. India, in the last few months has been talking to the Myanmarese government and it will now take up what constitutes another very significant milestone in its Look East Policy which is the building of the Sittwe port which is on the western coast of Myanmar. India is going to spend about 100 million dollars rebuilding this port and making the Kaladan river navigable. This will completely open a new access not only for the Northeast but also for the rest of India to the rest of Southeast Asia. In many ways what India is doing is to do a bypass surgery on Bangladesh. Bangladesh has been a major stumbling block in the process of regional integration. Until we are able to convince Bangladesh about the benefits of closer economic engagement with India, we have to think of alternatives and one major alternative is this new investment that India is about to make. This project will be launched in early 2007 and will take about three years to complete. There will be a modern port at Sittwe, the Kaladan river at Mizoram will be navigable and Northeast India will then have an alternative route for engagement. The Northeast will also have an alternative route for access to Myanmar and the rest of Asia. In addition to the Sittwe port there are a large number of highway projects that have been planned. In particular is the Asian Trilateral Highway which encompasses Thailand, Myanmar and Northeast India. This will result not only in road integration but integration of the transportation network of Asia and India. This will ultimately lead to a rail link from Kolkata to Hanoi via India's Northeast. This is a broad picture of what the Government of India has been thinking about, that in fostering this economic engagement with Asia lies not only new trade opportunities for India itself but also opens out new avenues for the development of India's Northeast.

As far as the Northeast is concerned we must accept the fact that in the years to come the future of the region lies in retaining its own unique cultural identity, in political integration with India and in economic integration with the rest of Asia. It is difficult to visualize such a model - a compartmentalized model, retaining your own cultural identity which is unique in many respects, political integration with the larger democratic system of India and economic integration with the larger economic body of ASEAN and the rest of Asia. This will call for a very creative political response both on the part of the decision makers of the Northeast and New Delhi and for this a lot of cobwebs that were built over the years, such as the Restricted Area Permit, limited telecommunication services and tight security regulations have to be removed. It is imperative to accept this model which is a three pronged model- a cultural identity of your own, political integration within the larger democratic framework of India but economic and commercial integration with Southeast Asia. This is a model that has been advocated for quite sometime and the Ministry of Commerce, Government of India has given it some operational content. It has been my endeavor to focus on key issues which I think are going to be very important in determining the pace and nature of this economic integration of India's Northeast to the rest of Asia. There is absolutely no doubt in my mind that the single most important requirement is infrastructure. Presently there is an enormous infrastructure deficit in India's Northeast and this is preventing paced economic integration. We must address this problem of infrastructure deficit in a very bold and business like fashion than we have been able to do in the past. This infrastructure covers roads, trading centers, land custom stations, power – it covers the entire gamut of physical infrastructure that is required in order to stimulate economic activity and promote trade integration. I have been impressing upon my colleagues in the state governments that we should work in a partnership mode in order to identify some of these key infrastructural bottlenecks and improve connectivity as part of this programme of development of the Northeast and its integration as part of India's Look East Policy.

The second major requirement is to make investments in economic activities that create surpluses for trade. Today the region can supply only a limited number of anthurium flowers and cannot meet the required demand. The region does not have the volume and quantity of pineapple, ginger and passion fruit that are required in the international market. Though Meghalaya is producing high quality tea it is unable to supply the quantity required. Similarly Manipur is growing high quality passion fruit and oranges. The question is, can the State produce the exportable and tradable surpluses required to be credible suppliers to the international markets? There is potential but having potential alone is inadequate. What is required is to have surpluses and the production capacity. Whether it is in the area of handicrafts or horticulture we need to make massive investments in creating production capacities which will create the surpluses that will be required for infrastructure. In the field of horticulture we have started a large number of projects. In Meghalaya we are looking at major investments in cultivating organic ginger and organic turmeric. Similarly in Manipur we have made major investments in mulberry silk, in Tripura it is rubber while in Assam it is tea. Each state has a unique resource endowment and it does not make sense for each state to compete with the others. Each state must specialize in something that is of unique characteristic to that state. Sikkim for example today has developed an international reputation for orchids. It does not make sense for other states of the Northeast to make major investments and try to cut in to the international markets for orchids. India this year has emerged as the second largest exporter of roses to the Japanese market. India has taken over Holland which used to be the second largest supplier of roses and today it is number two after South Korea. If adequate investments are made Meghalaya can be one of the most important exporters of cut flowers and roses to Japan. As a collective entity other state governments, other central government departments and institutions that have been created for the Northeast like the North Eastern Council must identify for each state a couple of unique projects which are suited to the resource endowments of that particular state and make major investments in creating production capacity, in creating the type of volumes that are required to create an international market presence. The Look East Policy will not be meaningful if we only keep looking. Looking east is for a purpose, to invest and generate revenue from the east. To fulfill this task India has to develop to be in a position to create those surpluses and those capacities which will make it a market power and strengthen its market presence. The Northeast cannot be a small supplier of anthuriums, citreous fruits, tea, ginger and retain the notion that the region has arrived on the international trading scale. The Asian Development Bank has recently completed a study of trade infrastructure in India's Northeast. It has identified three products available in the Northeast which can convert India's Look East Policy into product opportunity. They are pineapple, bamboo and rubber. The Government of India is in the process of looking at this report to identify the key areas of investment in these commodities to enable the Northeast to emerge as a major centre of production for the rest of Asia. This is essential so that the region can participate in the process of economic growth and economic prosperity that trade itself will bring.

A big stumbling block for getting new investment into the region is the reluctance of investors to come and invest in the Northeast. It is always a paradox- here is a region where the literacy is very high, the people are familiar with the English language and young men and women are noted for their enthusiastic embrace of new ideas. Yet somehow India's Northeast has not derived the benefits of increased investments. Today the government is not the sole investor in a region's investment. There is need to create a conducive atmosphere where private investment can be harnessed whether it is in information technology, education, horticulture or any other area. Unfortunately for a number of political reasons and for reasons having to do with the perception of violence, militancy and insurgency, private investments that should have come into the Northeast have not. The only exception is the cement industry in Meghalaya because of the tax incentives that are being offered. Meghalaya has suddenly become a major centre for the manufacture of cement including Assam. In fact 92% of all the investment that has taken place in the Northeast in the last fifteen years is only in the States of Assam and Meghalaya. However it is that small region in both these states that has been able to attract private investment which is largely concentrated in the mineral sector and in the cement industry. The ability of state governments to sell their states as investment destinations is going to be critical and part of this is going to depend on the states' ability to convince the investment community, for investment will ultimately be driven by sentiment. If the prevailing sentiment is that it is not a safe place to invest in the Northeast then no investor will be willing to take the risk. This is a Herculean task, it requires the central government's role and it requires the state governments to also play a pro-active role. It is imperative to make a determined effort to leverage on the unique strengths of the Northeast. The unique strengths of the Northeast are the ability to speak English, a youthful population and a population that is highly literate. These are the ingredients of success in a modern environment. If the central government were to make major investments in improving connectivity and infrastructure these initiatives will send a clear signal to investors to come and invest in the region. It will be the endeavor of the Ministry of Commerce, Government of India to work with all the state governments to convey this message to the larger investment community that while you may have instances of ethnic unrest such disturbances should not dissuade you from investing in the Northeast. There is no place in India which is free from violence. To develop the Northeast requires a close coordinated effort between the state governments and the central government. Investment summits for the Northeast should be held in the region. Such initiatives will be a systematic effort to sell the Northeast as an investment destination to investors from across India and from across the world particularly in those areas which have a comparable advantage- horticulture, handicrafts and information technology in particular.

It is of concern to note that the region suffers from a basic structural malaise. Every year the central government sends about fifteen thousand crores of rupees to the eight northeastern states for a population of about 30 million. This amounts to about five thousand rupees per person. If bank accounts were to be opened in the name of every poor person and the central government sends a cheque to each person, poverty would have been abolished in the region. The real question that needs to be addressed is where is this money going? It is common knowledge as to where this money finally parks. Money is not a constraint in the Northeast, the central government has ample funds to invest in the region's development. What is really lacking in the region is the ability to spend money in a manner that brings benefit to the people of the Northeast. All those involved in this chain of investment are benefited (including those who operate outside the region) except the people of the Northeast. Today the Right to Information has been put into operation. It is a very powerful right. One unique feature of the Northeast is that civil society is very powerful. It is important for people especially the youth and college students to use the right to information in demanding accountability from their political representatives. Ask them where is the fifteen thousand crores of rupees going? Where are the projects, where are the roads? Though money has been sanctioned yet the projects do not see the light of day. Such anomalies continue and there is a very simple explanation for this: people in Delhi do not have the time to get involved in the complexities of the Northeast, their conscience is salvaged by putting in more money. Whenever there is a problem in the Northeast, New Delhi comes up with a new package. There have been four Prime Minister's packages for the Northeast in the last ten years. Until we create infrastructure in the Northeast, unless we see public expenditure benefiting the people of the Northeast, unless we begin to see power, roads, transportation, markets (as these are some of the basic ingredients of trade infrastructure) we will not see the progress and development of the region. The single most important area of reform is accountability on public expenditure. If civil society, if educational institutions, if faith based organizations are able to use the right to information to demand from the political class and political establishment accountability and responsiveness then the people of the region will begin to see the emergence of a new Northeast.

The Look East Policy is a venture in which the entire civil society has a stake. Unless civil society begins to build a partnership on this model, unless we begin to create space for each other, unless we begin to recognize what is our individual responsibility we will not be able to do full justice to the Northeast. It is equally essential that we need not just the Look East Policy but also and more importantly we need the Look Northeast Policy so that we are able to harness the undoubted economic potential of this region and give to the people of this region the vision, the prospect of a better future.

Thank you.

CHAIRPERSON'S ADDRESS

J.D. Rymbai

Hon'ble Union Minister of State for Commerce, Shri Jairam Ramesh, former Speaker of the Lok Sabha and Member of Parliament Shri P.A. Sangma, former Union Minister of State for Commerce and Civil Aviation (Independent charge) Shri Rajiv Pratap Rudy, Professor D.P. Tripathi, National General Secretary, Nationalist Congress Party, Dr. D. Wanswett, Principal, Synod College, Dr. Merostar Rani, Coordinator, I.Q.A.C., distinguished dignitaries, delegates and all present

I am deeply humbled by this awesome experience of addressing this gathering of intellectuals who have traversed great distances, braving the onset of winter to converge in this august house, urged on by a keen interest in and a deep concern for the economic development of Northeast India in particular which concurrently has been given a fillip by the Look East Policy initiated by the Government of India to examine fresh avenues for trade and commerce with our Southeast Asian neighbors.

On behalf of the State of Meghalaya, I warmly welcome all outstation resource persons and participants to this land of many hues of nature and assure you all of our celebrated hospitality. I must congratulate Synod College for taking on this challenging venture of organizing a national level seminar on a theme that will determine not only the economic future of east India, particularly the Northeast because of its unique strategic geo-political importance to the rest of the country, but also the policy's growing implications in the political and other impressed areas. As you are aware the Look East Policy launched in 1992 had its origin in the end of the Cold War, following the disintegration of the Soviet Union and the emergence of the USA as a super power. In the aftermath of India's liberalization it was more than just a foreign policy alternative as it provided a development alternative as well, in synchronization with globalization and resurgence of Asia as an economic powerhouse. To quote the Hon'ble Prime Minister of India, Manmohan Singh, "*it was also a strategic shift in India's vision of the world and India's place in the evolving global economy*". Though the policy was given an initial thrust with the then Prime Minister (Late) Narasimha Rao visiting China, Japan, South Korea, Vietnam and Singapore, and India becoming a sectoral dialogue partner with the Association of South East Asian Nations (ASEAN) in 1992, the policy was pursued in good earnest till only recently. I appreciate this endeavor of Synod College to redraw our attention to this policy and step on the pedal for it to be carried forward in an effective manner. It is only in the beginning of the twenty-first century that India has given a big push to this policy when it became a summit-level partner of ASEAN in 2002 and was simultaneously involved in regional initiatives such as the Bay of Bengal Initiative for Multi-Sectoral Technical and Economic Cooperation (BIMSTEC) and the Mekong-Ganga Cooperation (MGC), and now finally becoming a member of the East Asia Summit in December 2005.

A close look at the policy reveals that it was not meant only to improve relations with Southeast Asia but there were a number of dimensions too. The post-Cold War political atmosphere offered an opportunity to frame a policy initiative by expanding the scope considerably to include political as well as economic aspects which came to be known as the Look East Policy. Since then it has become a multi-faceted policy with a multi-pronged approach to establish strategic links with as many countries as possible, establish institutional linkages with ASEAN, and develop strong economic bonds with eastern neighbors. The policy was also meant to be an attempt to carve a place for India in the larger Asia Pacific region, economically the most vibrant region. Yet another intention was to highlight India's economic potential for investment and trade. The best aspect of renewed engagement between India and ASEAN is that now both recognize that each has something to offer to the other. The ASEAN region has an abundance of natural resources, manufacturing abilities and technological skills that can provide a natural base for the growth of synergies and integration between ASEAN and India. The policy has acquired new dimensions and expanded to include new key areas that have led the organizers of this Seminar to invite learned experts and scholars to look at it afresh and discover new meaning and implications.

While wishing all fruitful deliberations at the Seminar and pleasant stay in Shillong, I express my confidence that at the end of the day, the policy will have been given a new thrust and new approaches and new areas identified for it to be increasingly important and beneficial to all impacted by it.

Once again, I wish the Seminar success in all its aspects.

Thank you

1

INTRODUCTION

Editors

I

Northeast India has received abundant attention over many decades the reasons for which are numerous. The progression of development and its bearing on the people of the region have been a recurrent theme in the consideration of the government, non-governmental organizations and professionals. Initiatives have been set in motion to realize the myriad sentiments and aspirations of the people of the region. Much remains to be accomplished if the region and its people are to savor the resources and endowments that they so abundantly enjoy.

Southeast Asia did not escape the wrath of intervening external powers and gory ideological wars. Regional security witnessed a transformation at the fag end of the cold war with the disintegration of the former USSR. The closure of the first Soviet military bases in Vietnam and later those of the United States of America in the Philippines in the early 1990's could be construed as the beginnings of a new Southeast Asia. Regional players emerged to vie for influence in an atmosphere of transition from a bipolar to a multi polar world. The Look East Policy emerged under such conditions when India decided to look within Asia to establish itself as a formidable economic Asian power. This policy was also the effect of India's attempt to deregulate its economy by ushering in a climate of liberalization. Thus the Look East Policy was simultaneously launched with India's liberalization policy following a thaw in Southeast Asia's ideological orientations. It was initiated as a development strategy aimed at accelerating India's engagement with its eastern international neighbors. Under the then Prime Minister Narasimha Rao India took a decision to significantly engage with ASEAN. At the fourth ASEAN Summit held in Singapore in January 1992, ASEAN Heads of Government agreed to establish sectoral dialogue on trade, investment and tourism with India. Since then there has been no looking back and sub-regional cooperation between India and its neighbors has paved the way even for multi-lateral relations. A crucial aspect of the Look East Policy will be India's ability to engage with its neighbors through its eastern land bridge along the international borders with Nepal, Bhutan, the autonomous region of Tibet in China, Myanmar and Bangladesh. The Northeast is significantly placed in the focal point of this policy.

The Northeast region comprises of the eight states of Assam, Arunachal Pradesh, Manipur, Meghalaya, Mizoram, Nagaland, Sikkim and Tripura. It covers an area of 2,55,000 sq. kms. which constitutes about 7.9% of the total geographical area of the sub-continent. This region is richly endowed with natural and mineral resources and has been identified as one of the world's biodiversity hotspots. It is home to a population of 39 million (2001 census) diverse and remarkable in culture and tradition, with 80% of this population living in the countryside. Yet this diverse composition has also been a bane to unity and prosperity with demands ranging from ethnic assertion to political independence. Verghese has aptly described the region as a "*rainbow country: extraordinarily diverse and colourful, mysterious when seen through parted clouds, a distant and troubled frontier for all too many*".[1]

The implementation of the Look East Policy has inevitable implications for the northeast region. The policy has been envisaged to achieve growth and development for the region. It is intended to initiate industrial development in an industrially deficient region, diversification of industrial activity, employment generation and trade and market expansion in accordance with the potentials of the region. To be inclusive the realities must match the objectives to be achieved. A number of pertinent questions arise: Will the northeast gear itself to develop exportable surpluses in commodities that are in demand in the international market? Is the region willing to engage itself in resolute economic association with Southeast Asia or will it remain only a "corridor"? These are questions that have no immediate answers. The Look East Policy is an initiative in motion, its results will not immediately be visible especially in a region that has been weighed down by numerous concerns. Jairam Ramesh has appropriately remarked that cobwebs need to be cleared if the Look East Policy is to benefit the Northeast.

It should be the endeavor of the Look East Policy to harness the huge human resource of the northeast where 'employability' rather that employment generation should be the key focus. Similarly if the policy is to take concrete shape good governance should be a key element of the northeastern states. Transparency, accountability and timely execution of projects should reflect their commitment to implementing the policy. They should demonstrate the qualities of responsive administration, administration that is corruption free, continuously in touch with people's needs and accessible at all times. If development is to flow to the citizens it should be people centric, gender neutral, participatory and adopt a 'bottom- up' planning approach. The Look East Policy should stimulate the Northeast to the path of economic well being and prosperity. It should strive to eliminate the perpetual dependency syndrome that has been engendered in the region. It should usher in an impression of self confidence to shape the region's destiny in the face of emerging opportunities.

II

This book is a collected work of the deliberations and papers that were presented at the national seminar "Look East Policy: Impact on Northeast India". The deliberations were interesting as they did not strictly adhere to an academic or intellectual milieu but also embraced field observations of those who were or have been engaged in carrying this policy forward. The first set of presentations address wide-ranging issues that are pertinent to the Northeast. In his paper *The Face of the Northeast*, D.P. Tripathi firmly calls for the need to remove prejudices that have been associated with the Northeast. He observes that a new class of young professionals with a new idiom of life has emerged in the region. It is this class, he firmly believes, that will play a decisive role in societal transformation. P.A. Sangma in his paper *Initiating Transformation in Northeast India* observes that concrete measures and initiatives will enable the region to stand on its own and shed the dependency syndrome. He stresses on the importance of establishing a single think tank and single funding agency to streamline the development process. He also calls upon the young, educated and dedicated people to participate in the political process. In *An Agenda for the Northeast* R.P. Rudy inquires into the contributions that have been made by the Northeast. He suggests giving the region an alternative nomenclature to inculcate in the people a sense of belongingness. He also suggests with conviction that if given the opportunity the Northeast will definitely be able to perform and achieve in the various indicators to economic prosperity.

The second set of presentations address issues significant to trade, commerce and the role of financial institutions. In their joint paper *India's Look East Policy: Economic Possibilities for the Northeast* Amiya Sarma and Bhupen Kumar Sarma examine initiatives that have been undertaken under the Look East Policy. This paper makes suggestions to harness the potential benefits that will accrue from an improved economy of the Northeast. B.P. Muktieh's paper *Role of Financial Institutions and Banks* briefly examines the emergence of the Look East Policy initiative and its implications for the Northeast. The paper also suggests measures through which financial institutions can play an effective role in implementing the policy. In her paper *Border Trade of Northeast India with Bangladesh: Impacts and Potential* I. Wanswett examines the reasons that facilitate border trade. The paper suggests ways to enhance the economic relations between the Northeast and her international neighbors especially Bangladesh. It also examines the impact of informal trade on the region's economy. Lambodar Rout's paper on *Look East Policy: Meghalaya's Coal Trade with Bangladesh* examines the emergence of coal trade between Meghalaya and Bangladesh. It discusses the export procedures and examines the bottlenecks that arise in facilitating trade along the Indo-Bangladesh border with special focus on the Dawki land custom station. The paper *Regional Economic Cooperation between India and ASEAN: Trade Opportunities for the Northeast Region* jointly presented Ratul Mahanta and Daisy Das discusses the initiatives that have been taken to promote regional cooperation between India and ASEAN. The paper makes a plea for development of physical linkages to enhance trade between the two.

The third set of presentations address issues significant to promoting tourism. In *Endorsing Tourism: A Resource for the Northeast* Charles Reuben Lyngdoh briefly discusses the meaning of the term 'tourism'. The paper highlights key areas of tourism which can be promoted in the Northeast – rural tourism, medical and health tourism, MICE tourism and Christmas tourism. He suggests the need for states to come forward with world record breaking events in order to attract visitors to the region. Mousumi Borah in her paper *Look East Policy: Promoting Tourism in the Northeast* emphasizes on the need to encourage the promotion of tourism in the Northeast through an integrated tourism policy involving all stakeholders of the region. The paper highlights the importance of tourism as an instrument to economic development while suggesting measures to improve the present scenario. In her paper *Sustaining Tourism through the Look East Policy* Sangita Kakoty discusses India's paced economic engagement with its eastern neighbors. The paper stresses on the importance of promoting tourism to show case the region's natural endowments. The paper adequately highlights the probable dangers of promoting tourism in the absence of a careful assessment of its probable impact on resources and communities.

The presentations are attempts to reexamine the Northeast through the Look East Policy and offer suggestions as to the best possible ways of engaging the region through this nascent and emerging development strategy.

REFERENCE

1. Verghese, B.G.: *India's Northeast Resurgent* (4th edn.), Konark Publishers, New Delhi, 2004 cited in *NIPFP Vision Document 2020*.

2

THE FACE OF THE NORTHEAST

D.P. Tripathi

The Look East Policy is a policy of discussion and of immense interest for the people of Northeast India. It is my desire to share some thoughts about the Look East Policy, its implementation and possibilities as far as the over all growth of the Northeast is concerned. The famous scientist Albert Einstein had appropriately remarked that it is easier to split an atom than to split a prejudice. For the development of the Northeast and for the proper implementation of the Look East Policy, the prejudices both internal (those that exist within the region amongst the various ethnic groups, amongst the various components of society) and the prejudices about this region that prevail in New Delhi and other parts of the country have to be broken down effectively. Napoleon Bonaparte had once said that there is no ability without opportunity. If given an opportunity the quality of development, the entire approach and vision about social change undergoes a decisive transformation. How many years did it take to establish one central North Eastern Hill University in Meghalaya? If opportunity is given then change is immediately visible. To cite another example, the Assamese people in spite of the numerous problems that they face have been able to produce world class literary figures from Birendra Kumar Bhattacharya to Mamoni Raisom Goswami. If one looks at these developments holistically then there are great possibilities. How many years did it take the centre to allocate a cabinet berth to a representative of the tribal people? It took decades, until Purno A. Sangma was finally made a minister. Once opportunity is given then ability also follows. This is the kind of prejudice, this is the kind of total lack of vision that needs to be removed.

What has happened in the last two decades in the Northeast the problems of insurgency and inter ethnic strife notwithstanding, is the emergence of a new class which however has not been given adequate attention and analysis. The last two decades have seen the emergence of a professional class of young men and women who are highly educated and motivated, visible not only in India but in distinguished institutions in the United States of America and Europe. This class is slowly but steadily emerging in the Northeast. Today there are about 15000 students from the Northeast pursuing their studies in Delhi alone. Similarly in Pune there are about 8000 students from the Northeast. This new class of young men and women that is emerging has different dreams and different desires and therefore an entirely new idiom of life. This is going to be their greatest strength for an overall change in the Northeast whether it is the Look East Policy, economic integration with Southeast Asian countries and neighbors or political integration with India. This class will keep away from taking to guns for short term reasons. This class is more interested like other Indian middle classes in economic development, peaceful existence and quality life. This class is the greatest strength of the Northeastern region and it is going to play a very decisive role in implementing not merely the Look East Policy but also societal transformation of the region. There is a lot of talk about insurgency in the Northeast. However there is nearly 24% of Indian territory which is controlled by the Maoists. Today the Maoists have come under one banner. The question arises, is there no investment or development in these areas under the control of the Maoists? The answer is no, investment and economic development is still taking place in these areas where the Maoists are predominantly active. Taking a queue out of the Northeast the State of Mizoram today is an appropriate example of tranquility and harmony from this region, a State that has transformed itself from insurgency to harmony. Secondly Mizoram is perhaps the one State in India where elections are least expensive. Civil society and church organizations exercise their authority to ensure that electoral expenses are low and cheap while civil society is kept strong. Do the national media highlight this face of Mizoram to the rest of the country? These are the issues that need to be highlighted to the rest of the country about the Northeast. Sikkim is another State which has today become a model of peace and growth. From the experiences of neighbors in the vicinity, the Northeast needs to develop certain centers. The Lokapriya Gopinath Bordoloi International Airport located in Guwahati is in the list of those airports which will be modernized and it will be converted into one of international standards by the Ministry of Civil Aviation. The work is time bound, it will commence by March 2007 and will be completed by March 2009. Once policy perspective changes there is need to develop and improve according to this perspective. Shillong can very well emerge as a great centre for education not only for the Northeast but also for students coming from the neighboring countries.

The need of the hour is to create a congenial milieu and from that environment to develop a kind of integrated social structure. Development is to be found in an environment where civil society is strong. In this factor the Northeast has many great distinctions to offer. It is also important to note that society gets the government it deserves. It is social change that brings in political change all over the world. Therefore for any kind of delight in this region a new light is necessary. Horticulture and handicraft are two areas that have immense potential in the Northeast. It is my opinion and suggestion that the Union Agricultural Ministry should hold a summit at Shillong with all the north eastern horticulture ministers on horticulture development for the entire Northeast. It is important for the ministry to devise a time bound framework for investment and development in this sector.

To conclude I quote the words of Dylan Thomas who said that when there are turbulent times, when you have to see that new light has to be protected,

> "*Do not go gentle into that good night*
> Old age should burn and rave at close of day
> *Rage, rage against the dying of light*".

3

INITIATING TRANSFORMATION IN NORTHEAST INDIA

P.A. Sangma

This question had been put to us at the Seminar, "every year the Government of India gives Rs 15000 crores to the states of the Northeast". Where is that money going? This is a very big question and it is imperative that we answer it. There is an old Chinese saying that if you want to help a hungry man don't give him fish to eat, teach him the art of catching fish.

> *"Give me fish and I eat for a day, teach me to fish and I eat for a lifetime".*

This saying is the answer to the question put before us. The Government of India has for so long been giving us fish to eat. It has not taught us the art of catching fish. Therefore what is required today is to teach us the art of catching fish so that we can stand on our own feet. It is not realistic for the Northeast to perpetually depend on the centre. This is where the objection lies. Everyone from the Northeast in unison should speak in one voice and ask the Government of India to provide concrete measures and initiatives that will enable the people of the region to stand on their own.

The Look East Policy has been a policy under consideration since 1992. My concern is that it is not enough to only look east but to also go east and engage oneself in numerous activities. To cite the example of China one may ask how has China applied this phrase "*to teach one the art of catching fishing*"? Have they really followed their own wisdom? The answer is yes. Yunnan one of China's southern provinces is a mirror of India's Northeast – historically underdeveloped, geographically isolated and like the Northeast is far from the capital Beijing. It is home to 26 diverse ethnic groups different in culture and language and it has also witnessed insurgency movements. Yunnan is the 8th largest Chinese province. It comprises an area of 3,94,000 square km covering 4.1 % of the whole territory of China. Approximately 84% of its territory is rugged mountain, 10% highland and hills and 6% lowland and valleys. Yunnan is one of the most culturally diverse places in the world. The geographical diversity of the region has enabled the development of the distinct life-styles, customs, religious beliefs and social structures of Yunnan province's different ethnic groups. Each group also has its own colorful costumes, crafts, dances, music and songs. However the kind of secessionist movements that are visible in India are also present in Yunnan. What has the government done? It set up an International Regional Cooperation Office to focus on a very clear development strategy for Yunnan. This is what is missing in the Northeast of India – a very clear development strategy. Take the example of the Stilwell Road that travels 61 kms through India, 1033 kms through Myanmar and about 632 kms in China. This 632 kms in China has become a multi-lane international highway. What about the 61 kms in India? It takes almost 3 hours to travel this stretch. China had earmarked 2.5 billion US dollars to develop cross border roads in Myanmar stretching about 1040 kms.

The Government of India allocates 15000 crores a year

for the Northeast. The question is how is this money sent to the Northeast? This amount is chanelized through a number of agencies - Planning Commission allocation to various states in the Northeast, central government ministries allocation, centrally sponsored projects particularly rural development, North Eastern Council, DoNER Ministry, Ministry of Tribal Affairs and so on. And how is this money allocated? One crore in one project, two crores in another and this is how the funding pattern is interspersed. It is for this reason that no development is visible. There are too many funding agencies and the financial allocation is too thinly spread. What is important is visibility. There should only be one funding agency in the country. Financial allocation should be invested in projects which are visible and this will have an impact on the downstream effect of employment generation. Though there are many funding agencies, planning agencies are absent. There is no think tank and there are no institutional think tanks in the Northeast. In Yunnan besides a provincial government there is also an International Regional Cooperation Office. Yunnan is very interested in India, a lot of research has also been done on the Northeast of India. In fact there is the Yunnan Development Research Centre, the Yunnan Development Strategy Centre and the Yunnan Social Science Academy. However similar agencies are absent in the Northeast. This is the need of the hour, the setting of such research centres as think tanks to policy initiatives.

The outcome of this seminar has immense significance. As political representatives of the region we should address these issues on the floor of the House in Parliament, in the various Parliamentary Committees, in the various seminars that are conducted all over the country. This initiative of Synod College should endeavor to be the beginning of a think tank process, the beginning of a think tank exercise paving the way for a clear cut direction addressing the Northeast's concerns on development. What we need is a single think tank and a single funding agency. The North Eastern Council should discontinue to be a funding agency. It is my strong recommendation that the North Eastern Council should become a think tank for this region. An appropriate nomenclature may also be thought of for this proposed institution – the Northeast Infrastructure Development Authority or the Northeast Infrastructure Development Council. The scheme of things within the present functioning of the North Eastern Council compels even a Member of Parliament to make meager, insignificant requests for road repairs and so on. In a globalized world today it is true that much of the initiative should come from the state governments. In a small State like Meghalaya what does our planning body comprise of? The State Planning Board of Meghalaya has one Chairman, two or three co-Chairmen and Vice Chairmen. The members include those persons who could not become ministers or those candidates who lost the last elections, political leaders who could not be given party posts. The State Planning Board which is supposed to be the brain of Meghalaya has become a rehabilitation centre for disgruntled politicians. How is the State to progress? The Commerce Minister at the centre has at least a dozen advisers who are highly distinguished economists, professors and professionals. However in the case of the State of Meghalaya one rarely finds distinguished economists as advisers to the Chief Minister.

Times have changed and we also need a change of political leaders. We need to look for young, dedicated and educated people to participate in the political process. We need young people who are up-to-date with the changes taking place in the world, up-to-date with new technology and new knowledge. As a State we also have to change our own image and shoulder the responsibility of performing. Political representatives need to perform better and the State urgently needs a think tank. It should be the endeavor of educational institutions such as Synod College to step in and fill this vacuum. As an example, in Europe all the policy measures are researched by the universities. Similarly any new governmental policy that is announced by the President of America is announced from a university campus and not from a party meeting or a public meeting. This approach reflects the collective thinking of the intellectuals of the country. These are important practices that need to be considered.

4

AN AGENDA FOR THE NORTHEAST

Rajiv Pratap Rudy

Looking at the gathering I must say that Synod College has effectively balanced the political quorum of the seminar on the Look East Policy by inviting speakers from different political parties. Having been a former minister myself I do not wish to address the structured aspects of the Look East Policy, the documents of which I have had access to. However it is the informal structure of the Policy that I wish to dwell upon.

For years the term, "northeastern states" has been in common usage, a term used as if the region is a part of some north western frontier province or some isolated part of the country. Intellectuals must give this region a better nomenclature which inculcates in its people the sense of belongingness. Similarly alternative names could be used while speaking about the region. A committee could be created to consider alternative terms which give the region more dignity and more reflection than the present term does. What have the northeastern states offered to India? When the Government of India and the Ministry of Environment and Forests speaks about the 33% forest cover that is required to keep the ecological balance in the country it is the Northeast which provides that average. If the forest cover of the

Northeast were to be removed from the present average the forest cover of the rest of the country will only be around 3-4%. This region acts as a buffer, a protective defense mechanism to the rest of the country as it is surrounded by other countries. The Northeast protects the country, it offers soldiers and officers to the armed forces of the country- a great human resource assigned to the country's defense. It has immense potential for generating hydro electric power the cost of which is much more than fifteen thousand crores. To take an example, the cost of constructing a dam in Uttaranchal will not be less than two lakh crores. If the Union Government has given the Northeast fifteen thousand crores and does not see the results then it should enquire as to why the results are not visible. Politicians are not to be blamed for every lapse of implementation. If P. A. Sangma who headed the coal ministry and a loss making organization is able to convert it to a profit making organization, it definitely shows the capacity of the Northeast. It is an opportunity given - the opportunity which comes to you will define your ability. The Northeast has not been given an opportunity. The day the region is given an opportunity its performance will certainly be visible. Why are the same questions being repeated year after year - that delivery is not taking place, the region suffers from poor infrastructure, low capital investment, unemployment, poor education and insurgency when we should actually be looking for solutions to these problems. What is the action plan of the Union Government? I do not subscribe to the view that it should be left to the states to develop themselves. These are questions that need to be pondered over and addressed. Development will occur naturally in concurrence with a larger vision set. In the aviation sector what happened in the economy that suddenly brought down the air fares? It was the policy decision of the Government of India to create a market economy, to create certain policy changes which ensured that the monopoly of a few operators was broken and competition was ushered in.

Why did Mumbai become the financial capital of this country? It became the financial capital of this country because the British then had decided to make it a gateway of India. The British developed the finest port at Mumbai and created that infrastructure which made it the hub of the western sector and the focal nodal entrance point to the country. In this way Mumbai automatically became the country's financial capital. Taking a larger reference, why is England treated as the financial hub of Europe? It is due to the fact that today the aviation hub for the entire Europe is Heathrow airport. The very fact that it became the hub of all flight operations going to the Far East, Europe and the Americas, England automatically became the financial hub as well. In a similar vein it is essential to make Guwahati and Shillong the hub of international transport in this country, to enable this region to carry its goods and services to the Far East. There is need to decide fundamental policy at the intellectual level. If the Union Government is insecure, weak, and incapable of handling situations and issues because it has set inadequate policies, it will never allow the Northeast to emerge.

As responsible political representatives we should never entertain the idea that the Northeast will be cut off from main land India. It will remain very much a part of this country. We have the moral strength, we have the personalized strength, we have the cultural strength to never ever expect the Northeast to leave this country. There is need to create a hub of development in the Northeast, to increase production and exports and to ensure that the region is self reliant and self dependent. At a certain point of time the southern states of Karnataka, Tamil Nadu and Kerala did feel neglected by the central government. However today they are some of the most progressive states of the country. They have the best resources, the best manpower resources and they decided to develop themselves. This is what is required in the Northeast a region having huge potential in manpower, finesse and the advantage of fluent spoken English. The states of the Northeast have to take the decision to do things for themselves and reduce their dependence on others. The states have to start looking for leadership within themselves and develop the same, this is the desire that should emerge. If they can show this vision it will mark the beginning of their survival. The locational advantage that the Northeast has to engage in market relations with Southeast Asia is phenomenal. We need radical policy changes at the centre as far as the Northeast is concerned. The central government should not harbor misconceptions about this region.

Much needs to be done many issues need to be taken up by focused people in the government. When the situation is favorable we will sit again and complete the unfinished vision that we have for the Northeast.

5

INDIA'S LOOK EAST POLICY: ECONOMIC POSSIBILITIES FOR THE NORTHEAST

Amiya Sarma & Bhupen Kumar Sarma

Introduction

The Look East Policy introduced by the Government of India in the nineties was basically a strategy to change its foreign policy in accordance with the changed world business scenario. This policy had its genesis in the end of the cold war following the collapse of the Soviet Union. It is an attempt to integrate India with her neighboring eastern economies. Even when India's approach to development was inward looking and state controlled some smaller countries to its east had emerged as strong economies and came to be known as the 'Asian Tigers'. The performance of these economies finally compelled policy makers in India to look eastward for inspiration for rapid economic development. The Look East Policy is one of the important strategies of India's development. Implementation of this policy will certainly impact upon the economy of the Northeast. The northeastern region of India is a geographically isolated area which is linked to the rest of the country through a 'chicken neck' at Siliguri in West Bengal. For better part of the post-independence period the region had a peripheral existence in the Indian economy. With the initiation of the Look East Policy this region has become a focal point. It is expected that the successful implementation of this policy will bring certain economic benefits to the Northeast region (hereinafter NER).

Brief Background of Look East Policy

After independence India was attracted to the tremendous development achieved by western countries. It had been recognized that the noteworthy factor behind the rapid economic development of these countries was the process of industrialization. India was inspired by the concept of economic planning which particularly prevailed in the economy of the erstwhile Union of Soviet Socialist Republics (hereinafter USSR). Accordingly India initiated five year plans from 1951 onwards the prime aim of which was rapid economic growth of the country through industrialization. One of the main objectives of planning was to attain self-reliance which is possible only when a country is able to produce everything domestically. Two types of trade strategies were sought to be promoted towards this end-strategy: import substitution and export promotion. Strategies of import substitution were generally designed to produce those commodities, which were previously imported from foreign countries, domestically. This trade strategy had two major objectives:

(a) to save valuable foreign exchange due to import of desired commodities.

(b) to achieve self-sufficiency in the production of as many imported items as possible.

On the other hand export promotion strategies were conceived to expedite the export sector. But due to export pessimism Indian policy makers decided to go for import substitution rather than export promotion.

These trade policies were unable to bring any significant contribution towards the economic growth of India. It is well known that in the 1980's problems such as a growing fiscal deficit, inflationary pressure and balance of payments crises became severe. As a result policy makers felt the need to change the development strategy. In this context the Indian Government introduced economic reform measures in 1991. These reform measures were both internal and external in nature. Through internal reforms the Indian economy was liberalized from excessive state control and a market-oriented approach was adopted. On the other hand external reforms paved the way for opening up the Indian economy to the global market. Thus greater integration of India with rest of the world economies was ensured through globalization. As part of the policy of globalization the policy of looking towards the countries in the east was encouraged. In this context a question arises, why did Indian policy makers not pay any attention to the eastern countries soon after independence? This was because the eastern countries were also underdeveloped like India. Japan was a developed nation and it was treated like any other developed western country. The emergence of Singapore, Taiwan, Hong Kong and Korea as powerful 'Asian Tigers' to the east did not inspire India to change her economic policy regime. But the economic prosperity achieved by countries like Thailand, Malaysia and Indonesia nearer home attracted India's interest. The spectacular growth of China's trade and liberalization policy since 1980s injected an intense desire to develop the Indian economy. Expanded and stronger trade relationships with the eastern countries were thought to be beneficial by the Indian Government in this regard. As a result policies such as the Look East policy assumed importance.

Policy Initiatives in Practice

To enhance economic cooperation with the eastern economies, the Government of India is trying to establish closer economic ties through increased trade relations. Accordingly, certain proposals have been made to form regional blocks so that preferred and free trade can be initiated with these countries.

BIMSTEC

As an endeavor to forge regional economic cooperation, a sub-regional grouping BISTEC was established on June 6, 1997 in Bangkok among the countries along the Bay of Bengal—Bangladesh, India, Sri Lanka and Thailand Economic Cooperation. Myanmar was an observer but joined this organization as a full member at a special ministerial meeting held in Bangkok on December 22, 1997 upon which the name of the organization was changed to BIMSTEC. In 2003 Bhutan and Nepal joined this group. This association seeks to increase economic cooperation between member countries in certain important areas such as trade, investment, fisheries, agriculture, transportation and human resource development. Its first summit was held on July 31, 2004 in which the grouping was renamed the Bay of Bengal Initiative for Multi-Sectoral Technical and Economic Cooperation. It was expected that the two Southeast Asian nations—Thailand and Myanmar would provide necessary linkages to other member nations to increase economic cooperation to the Association of South East Asian Nations (hereinafter ASEAN) and the East Asian countries. Effective implementation of India's Look East Policy depends upon closer relationship between India and the ASEAN. Greater economic ties with ASEAN can be ascertained through a good relationship between the Northeast and Myanmar since geographically this region and Myanmar share a common international border.

Kunming Initiative

Another effort to enhance regional cooperation with the eastern countries was the Kunming Initiative. A conference on Regional Cooperation and Development between Bangladesh, China, India and Myanmar (hereinafter BCIM) was held on August 17, 1999 in Kunming, the capital of Yunnan province in the southwest of China. An agreement for improving communication links among these countries called the Kunming Initiative was signed. The main thrust of the agreement was to request the concerned governments to develop adequate road, rail, waterway and air communication facilities between the southwestern region of China and the northeastern region of India. An attempt had also been made to revive the ancient southern silk route between Assam and Yunnan. As the northeastern region is located at the corner of India it can become the gateway of the country to the east expediting international trade between India and rest of the developing economies.

The Mekong-Ganga Cooperation Project

This project is another significant attempt to increase regional cooperation among India and the Southeast Asian nations. The project was approved between India and five Southeast Asian nations, namely Thailand, Vietnam, Laos, Cambodia and Myanmar on November 10, 2000 in Vientiane, the capital of Laos. The main aim of this project was to develop overland trade, tourism, communication and transport linkages including the East-West Corridor project and the Trans-Asian highway.

Importance of Myanmar

From India's point of view policies and cooperation of Myanmar have assumed importance for realizing the goals set up in the above mentioned initiatives. This is because of Myanmar's special geographical position as a meeting point between East and South Asia. Trade across the Indo-Myanmar border is not only significant to accelerate trade relations between India and Myanmar but to also help in creating closer economic ties with countries lying east and southeast of Myanmar. Though attempts have been made to expedite trade relations with Myanmar through initiatives such as reducing trade barriers some difficulties still exist from the Myanmarese side. The economic and commercial policy of the ruling military junta is out of touch with the liberalized economic regimes of the countries surrounding it. For instance Myanmar's currency, the *Kyat*, is grossly overvalued as per the official exchange rate. Since informal trade operates on the basis of the market driven unofficial exchange rate, such trade especially the import part will be unviable at the official rate. So unless Myanmar's currency is revalued more realistically, moving from informal to formal trade channels will be difficult. Experts are of the opinion that the present policy regime in Myanmar is not going to be sustainable for very long and rationalization of economic and commercial policy has to materialize sooner or later.[1]

Economic Consequences for the Northeast

The Northeast region is now considered an 'asset' by the rest of India rather than 'excess baggage' as perceived in the past. The important question before the Government of India is how to utilize this asset with proper planning.[2] The pre-requisite to use the region as an asset is to develop infrastructural facilities because the existing facilities are not adequate. However the Northeast region of India is facing developmental challenges due to its landlocked condition. As pointed out by B.G. Verghese this region is South Asia's third landlocked state along with Bhutan and Nepal.[3] Due to this landlocked condition the Northeast is lagging behind in terms of connectivity and market access to its neighboring countries. Prior to the advent of the British the Northeast was connected with other countries through routes like the Silk Road. Northeast India was on the southern trails of the Silk Road which connected the western region of China through Central Asia to the Mediterranean.[4] The history of the Northeast's trading activities along the southern Silk Road establishes the fact that the present remote and troubled condition of the region is not unchangeable. Successful implementation of the Look East Policy depends on undertaking various developmental projects by the Government of India to help establish better communication and transportation network in the region.

The following observations could be considered potential benefits that the Northeast could derive from the implementation of India's Look East Policy:

(a) Northeast India's participation in merchandise trade with its neighboring countries may not be very encouraging. But there is considerable scope of improving trade in certain local products such as tea, spices, handloom, bamboo and cane handicrafts. Improvement of quality is the necessary condition for these products to capture the foreign market and derive benefit from enhancing trade activities.

(b) It is observed that a substantial volume of informal trade is taking place along the Indo-Myanmar border. Illegal trade along the border has resulted in huge loss of revenue for the Government of India as well as for the state governments of the Northeast. The Look East Policy will help in legalizing informal trade along the border and encourage the trading partners to expand their business. In addition, legalization will also enable the concerned governments to earn revenue through collection of duties on imports and exports. If trade is to be encouraged the rates of such duties have to be modest. However if the volume of trade increases the revenue collection can be substantial. Currently this potential for generating revenue for the government is being pocketed by agents and corrupt officials in return for facilitating the illegal informal trade.[5]

(c) There are immense possibilities for the Northeast to enjoy the spin off effects from trade by developing certain service sectors like hospitality, transport and communication, storage, banking and insurance.

(d) There is ample scope for entrepreneurial development among the local people of the region which in turn will create a favorable environment for the establishment of hotels, restaurants and *dhabas* along transportation routes. To meet the increased demand for food items, establishment of animal husbandry and fishery farms will be accelerated. The prospect of developing the motor vehicle servicing industry and fuel agencies with state of the art amenities to cater to the needs of passenger and transportation vehicles will also be encouraging.

(e) A favorable impact may be expected from India's Look East Policy on the existing unemployment problem in the Northeast. Unemployed people will find profitable jobs in the above ventures that will help in solving to a certain extent the acute unemployment problem faced by the region.

(f) In the process of implementing the Look East Policy trade relations between India and other neighboring countries will expand. This expanded trade may take place either through the sea route or through the land route. If trade takes place through the sea route, northeastern states will not be able to derive any gain from trade. Realization of economic benefits by these states depends on trade taking place through the land route.

Conclusion

Improving the transport and communication system is an essential condition for successful implementation of the Look East Policy. Construction of all weather roads, connecting highways, rail stations and airports are the need of the hour. The Indian government and the state governments of the Northeast should take initiatives to develop roads and other infrastructural requirements. Coordination among the four transportation systems - road, rail, river and air is also necessary for deriving significant economic gain from the Look East Policy. India's Look East Policy is a significant step for economic development of the Northeast in particular and the country in general through better cooperation and closer trade relationship with the countries to the east. The region will face both opportunities and challenges in its development. As far as the opportunities are concerned, states of the Northeast may become major beneficiaries by producing quality local products having a high demand in the foreign market. At the same time improvement of various service sectors such as hospitality, transport and communication, storage, banking and insurance, motor servicing and fuel agencies are also supposed to provide relief to the poor economic condition endured by the region. The improvement of the service sector may also address the severe unemployment problem faced by this region to a certain extent. There is a possibility of properly utilizing the region's endowed and untapped natural resources. However India may face security challenges from pursuing liberal and free trade relations with the eastern countries. Apart from the China factor and insurgency, roads through Myanmar may be used to bring drugs, illegal migrants, infectious disease and small arms more easily than before. Improved roads may worsen India's HIV/AIDS crisis.[6] Though there are negative implications to the implementation of the Look East Policy, yet the policy has the potential to transform India's Northeast to a region of peace and economic prosperity by assessing and managing the risks that are associated with the policy. To realize this possibility the Government of India and the state governments of the region should come forward with a positive outlook and actively participate in making the policy a success.

REFERENCES

1. Bezbaruah, M.P.: "Trade across Indo-Myanmar Border: A Bridge for the North-East to Asian Prosperity", CENISEAS Papers, 2004.
2. Chasie, Charles: "Look East Policy: Pertinent Issues", *Assam Tribune*, March 20, 2006.
3. Baruah, Sanjib: "Between South and Southeast Asia: Northeast India and the Look East Policy", CENISEAS Papers, No. 4, 2004.
4. Baruah, Sanjib: *op.cit.*
5. Bezbaruah, M.P.: *op.cit.*
6. Baruah, Sanjib: *op.cit.*

Sources Cited

1. Kuppuswamy, C.S.: "India's Look East Policy: More Aggressive, Better Dividends", South Asia Analysis Group, http://www.saag.org/%5Cpaper1663.html.
2. Panagariya, Arvind: "India in the 1980s and 1990s: A Triumph of Reforms", *IMF Working Paper*, 2004.

6

ROLE OF FINANCIAL INSTITUTIONS AND BANKS

B.P. Muktieh

The Look East Policy launched in 1992 was an inevitable offshoot of the closing stages of the cold war following the collapse of the Soviet Union. The policy was kick started when the then Prime Minister Narasimha Rao visited China, Japan, South Korea, Vietnam and Singapore. This initiative culminated in India becoming a sectoral dialogue partner with ASEAN in 1992. Both India and ASEAN became increasingly conscious of the potential in enhanced political, economic and security cooperation. The two sides felt that the time was ripe tc jettison the irrelevant historical baggage of the cold war era and look to forge a new and dynamic partnership. Now that India was ready to embrace free market economies the ASEAN members could sense enormous potential in trade and investment ties with India. There were geo-political considerations as well with regard to the historical dominance of China in the region. There was also a realization that decision-making in India was largely politically driven and even economic ties were determined by political equations. With the reforms firmly entrenched and the attractions of the East Asian miracle beckoning, India saw immense potential for trade and investment by the simple expedient of forging closer economic ties with her eastern neighbors. The fledgling Look-East Policy was only pursued in fits and starts right through the 1990s. It was only in the beginning of the 21st century that India gave the policy a big thrust by becoming a summit level partner of ASEAN (2002), a member of the East Asia Summit (2005) and when India also got involved in regional initiatives such as the Bay of Bengal Initiative for Multi-Sectoral Technical and Economic Cooperation (hereinafter BIMST-EC) and the Mekong-Ganga Cooperation (hereinafter MGC). BIMSTEC has identified six sectors for focused cooperation. For each sector a lead country has been designated: Trade and Investment (Bangladesh), Technology (Sri Lanka), Transport and Communication (India), Energy (Myanmar), Tourism (India), and Fisheries (Thailand). A Framework Agreement with the aim of establishing a Free Trade Agreement (hereinafter FTA) has been signed in February 2004. The Mekong-Ganga Cooperation Project involves six nations (India, Myanmar, Thailand, Laos, Cambodia and Vietnam) and is aimed at the development of overland trade, tourism, communication and transport linkages. It may be noted that barring India the rest are member states of ASEAN. In addition India has also entered into a number of bilateral pacts and free trade agreements with Thailand, Malaysia, Indonesia, Myanmar, Singapore, Cambodia, Laos and Vietnam to facilitate trade, investment and economic cooperation. The implementation of these agreements is however slow and painstaking as there was resistance from the Indian industry which feared dumping of cheaper imports and the mandatory domestic political compulsions which inhibit the pace of the economic reforms. In this regard the FTA with ASEAN is currently in limbo on account of the disagreement on the number of negative list items. Notwithstanding these hiccups the Look-East

Policy has slowly but surely started yielding results on the economic, political and strategic fields. ASEAN and India appear to have developed a clearer vision of the future of their relationship. India became a member of the East Asia Summit in December 2005. The share of Asia in India's trade is the highest at 29.38% and growing at a healthy rate of 26% in fiscal 2006. To quote Prime Minister Manmohan Singh '*it was also a strategic shift in India's vision of the world and India's place in the evolving global economy*'.

Look East Policy and the Northeastern States

The Northeast region comprising of the eight states of India shares 98% of its borders (about 5000km) with neighboring countries and only 2% with mainland India. Therefore given this topography trade and economic ties with its immediate neighbors makes more economic sense than trade with the distant markets in other parts of the country. Historically and traditionally through the centuries there has been a natural exchange of people, goods and services between our Northeast and the countries of South and Southeast Asia. The pre-1991 restrictive and isolationist Indian economic policies with high tariff walls and regime of strict import licensing not only shut out imports from western countries but also barred trade and economic ties with its neighbors. This had an adverse impact on trade and on the economies of the north eastern states who share a large international border as it deprived them of their natural markets and access to products produced in the neighboring countries just across the border. Trade with the mainland effectively increased the landed cost of imports and exports into the region. The central government has tried to compensate for this high transport and logistic cost by providing some mitigants like transport subsidy, marginally concessional railways tariffs and so on. The Indian government also offered subsidies and concessions for setting up new industries in the Northeast region. These subsidies have however failed to offset the disadvantage of the region. The closed borders effectively make the region land-locked as it shares 98% of its borders with the neighboring countries with whom India's relations have not exactly been friendly. The closed borders along with the limited markets in the region failed to attract industries despite the subsidies and concessions from the government for locating new industries in the Northeast and availability of a rich source of minerals and hydrocarbon. The huge hydroelectric power potential of the region has also not been harnessed for the same reasons. The acute law and order problems in most of the states act as an effective deterrent to the setting up of industries. Consequently, the region has remained largely an agrarian economy with limited trading avenues. India's Look East Policy and economic liberalization were expected to change the Government of India's priorities in the Northeast region leading to greater economic activity, greater trade and commerce, frequent cultural exchanges and people-to-people interactions with the immediate neighbors in this region.

There has also been substantial increase in India's trade with Asia, thanks to the Look East Policy. The share of Asia in India's trade is now the highest and has increased from 12% in 1992-93 to about 29.38% in 2005-06. The growth rate of India's trade with Asia as a whole is 26% and with ASEAN countries 20% during the period 2005-06. India's trade with countries bordering the Northeast has also seen a dramatic expansion. This dramatic expansion of trade with Asia and India's eastern neighbors has had little or no impact on the Northeast. Most of this trade expansion has taken place through the seaports. India is Looking East, but so far, not through its land borders. The second phase of the Look East Policy is expected to deepen and bring within its fold India's far eastern neighbors including Japan, China, Australia and

New Zealand with the impending conclusion of the various FTAs and bilateral agreements. It is clear that in the days to come India will aggressively pursue closer trade and economic ties with its eastern neighbors and indications are that this time it will include trade through its land borders. The north eastern region will need to be a part of the economic ties and trade expansion strategy in the second phase of the 'Look-East Policy' and become a center of transit for trade on the eastern contiguous borders to usher in a new era of economic growth in the region.

The Way Ahead

On July 6, 2006 the original trade route through the Nathu La pass in Sikkim popularly known as the silk route was reopened after 44 years. India's Directorate General of Foreign Trade (hereinafter DGFT), Ministry of Commerce and Industry, Government of India has notified 29 items of export to China through this trade route, with China being allowed to export 15 products to India in turn. The reopening of the historic silk route has significant potential to boost the economies of both the northeastern region of India and western China by linking Tibet to the Kolkata Port. This smoothening process is likely to set off investment activities in Sikkim and the surrounding areas. Trade facilitation measures including removal of non-tariff barriers and up gradation of regional infrastructure particularly the 143 km road link between Siliguri and Nathu La via Gangtok will enhance bilateral trade with China through this route. Indo-Myanmar border trade is also set to expand with the opening of a land custom station in Mizoram. The Border Roads Organization (hereinafter BRO) has been entrusted with the task of constructing a land custom station estimated to cost five crore rupees at Zakhawthar which will become another gateway to ASEAN nations. Rih is the custom station on the Myanmar side. At present only one trade point exists at Moreh in Manipur, projected as India's gateway to Southeast

Asian countries where border trade has been taking place with neighboring Myanmar. Officially trade between the two countries at this border post is open but the lack of road communication and other facilities on both sides is preventing the volume of trade from increasing. It needs to be emphasized that the physical infrastructure required for facilitating trade and economic links between the Northeast and the neighboring countries is largely absent. Infrastructural bottlenecks and delays at border points add substantially to the transaction cost in international trade.

Bangladesh, India, Myanmar, Sri Lanka and Thailand came together and formed an economic association called BIMST-EC linking the littoral states of the Bay of Bengal and signed the Framework Agreement in February 2004. This economic grouping aims to promote rapid economic cooperation between members in key areas like trade, investment, tourism, fisheries, agriculture, transportation links and human resource development. As members of ASEAN, Myanmar and Thailand will be moving towards developing free trade ties. It is therefore important that India should move ahead in clinching free trade agreements with Bangladesh and Myanmar at the earliest. The way should be paved for BIMSTEC to move towards becoming a Free Trade Association. There is need for introducing a number of trade facilitation measures to promote border trade with Myanmar and Bangladesh, including transportation systems that allow cross-border movements of vehicles and the provision of auxiliaries like weigh bridges and cold storage facilities. Other non-tariff barriers need to be removed to increase the volume of trade through the borders. All this only increases the urgency for concluding free trade agreements with our eastern neighbors. For the Northeast to gain from India's Preferential Trade Agreements (hereinafter PTA) and FTA with the economies of the east, the key variables are transit arrangements, creation of new trade routes and custom check posts and easy visa regime thereby making it possible for traders, businessmen and transport operators to move in and out of the region. For this to be possible would require substantial investments in infrastructure, construction of highways and bridges, re-establishment of rail links and communication facilities.

Role of Financial Institutional and Banks

The closed and large international borders along with limited market opportunities in the region have failed to attract industries in spite of subsidies and concessions from the government and availability of an abundant supply of minerals and hydrocarbon resources. The huge hydroelectric power potential of the region has also not been harnessed for the same reasons. The acute law and order problems in most of the states further deter the establishment of industries. The few industries set up in the past have either closed down or are operating at low unviable capacities. It is only those industrial units which cater to local demands that are running satisfactorily today. Consequently, the region has remained largely an agrarian economy with limited trading avenues. The exposure of all India financial institutions and banks in the region are small compared to the rest of the country. The large percentage of non-performing loans in their books further deters fresh investments in the region. There is a need for improving infrastructure, creating a favorable investment climate and encouraging a healthy credit culture. This will facilitate a reversal of the current negative perception about the safety of investments in the region amongst investors and lenders. State governments and other stakeholders to the economic progress of the region will have to play an important role in this respect. The Look-East Policy has opened new vistas of hope for the states of the Northeast. It promises to open up the borders that will act as an engine of economic growth and make the region a center of transit for trade with the eastern contiguous borders. However, for this to happen a strong political will, implementation of the various FTA and substantial investments in infrastructure, construction of highways and bridges, re-establishment of rail links and communication facilities are required. The Shukla Committee on 'Transforming the North East' estimated such investment to exceed Ra 25,000 crore. Substantial investments are also required to harness the hydrocarbon and hydroelectric potential and to develop infrastructure for the vast river networks. Investments are also required to develop local industries utilizing the rich local mineral resources, to upgrade the technology and scale of operations of the existing industrial units, upgrade and scale up agricultural produce, upgrade the standard of education, skill sets, developing infrastructure in the health sector, telecommunication sector and other sectors as well. The level of investments required will be substantial and will be beyond the capability of local governments, financial institutions and banks. Strong political will is required on the part of both the centre as well as the states to bring about an enabling political and economic environment to facilitate flow of investments from international and national sources.

At the international level there are multilateral development banks like the World Bank and Asian Development Bank (hereinafter ADB) that provide financial support and professional advice for economic and social development activities in developing countries. The World Bank is the world's largest purveyor of development assistance and is a vital source of financial and technical assistance to developing countries around the world. The Asian Development Bank is a regional multilateral development financial institution set up with the prime objective of improving the welfare of the people in Asia and the Pacific. The World Bank and ADB together lent about $26 billion in fiscal year 2004 to developing countries. With the necessary political initiatives these multilateral agencies can be major sources of funding in the region for infrastructure, education and healthcare projects that require huge funding with a long gestation period. Their main instruments for providing assistance to member countries are policy dialogue, loans, technical assistance, grants, guarantees and equity investments.

The all India financial institutions like the Small Industries Development Bank of India (hereinafter SIDBI), the Export Import Bank (hereinafter EXIM Bank), the Industrial Development Bank of India (hereinafter IDBI) which has since converted into a bank but still retaining its developmental role and commercial banks have been financing infrastructure projects, industry, agriculture, trade and commerce in the region. With an enabling environment and larger markets on account of opening of international borders, trade and commerce will grow manifold and economically feasible and financially viable industrial units could be setup in which case financial institutions and banks can substantially increase their investments in the region. Financial institutions and larger banks have a large exposure to the infrastructure sector viz. power, roads and highways, ports and telecommunication networks in other regions of the country where proper project formulation and risk mitigants were put in place with active involvement of the central and state governments. The same may be replicated in the northeastern region. Typically financial institutions provide advisory services, term loans, guarantees and equity. Banks on the other hand besides providing term loans also offer other fund-based credit products such as cash credit, working capital demand loan, overdrafts, bills and export finance, and non-fund based facilities in the nature of Letter of Credits (hereinafter LCs), standby LCs, bid bond guarantees, performance guarantees, financial guarantees, deferred payment guarantees and so on as part of the overall financial package. They also provide advisory services, loan syndication and finance for overseas acquisitions, capital market products and a bouquet of other services.

The central government has also been instrumental in setting up a specialized financial institution for the region. The North Eastern Development Finance Corporation Ltd. (hereinafter NEDFi) has been specifically put in place for promoting economic activities in the region and for carrying out techno-economic appraisal, identification and financing of projects. Besides there are state-level financial institutions such as the Meghalaya Industrial Development Corporation, the Assam Industrial Development Corporation, the Assam Financial Corporation, the Tripura Industrial Development Corporation which have a feel of local conditions and have been set up to promote and finance industries in their respective states.

Thus the institutional framework for financing infrastructure, industries, agriculture, trade and commerce are already in place for projects that are economically feasible and financially viable. There is however a need for greater financial inclusion and provision of financial services in the region. A more efficient financial intermediation by itself can lead to economic growth. The financial institutions and banks have a big stake in the success of the Look-East Policy in the region as an expanding trade, industrial development and economic growth will improve their balance sheets and involvement in the region.

7

BORDER TRADE OF NORTHEAST INDIA WITH BANGLADESH: IMPACTS AND POTENTIAL

I. Wanswett

Border trade in general refers to the flow of goods and services across the international borders between countries. In this sense it is a part of normal trade flow through a standard EXIM framework of nations. However the economic, social and political implications of border trade are far deeper than normal trade that flows through the seas and airports. Border trade in modern times occupies an important place for a country whether it is in the economic, social or political aspects. Border trade involves the cross border exchange of

(a) goods produced outside the bordering region
(b) goods produced within the region and
(c) goods of a third country origin.

What is considered in border trade is not goods having an origin in a third country but goods of two countries sharing common boundaries and produced within the two countries alone.

Border trade is a tool of regional development especially for large country like India. Some of its regions are far away from national market hubs but closer to the international border markets. Thus, it is advantageous for these regions to develop border trade with such neighbors rather than trade with the distantly located national markets. Borders which were earlier neglected are today seen as gateways for access to markets of neighboring countries. Moreover, border trade is now viewed as an important vehicle for the development of the border areas.

Northeast Region: A Profile

The Northeast region includes the states of Arunachal Pradesh, Assam, Manipur, Meghalaya, Mizoram, Nagaland and Tripura. Recently the State of Sikkim has been included in this geographical categorization. The region covers an area of 2.55 lakh square kilometers accounting for 7.9 % of the total land space of the country. As per the 2001 census only 39 million people live in this region which amounts to about 3.8 percent of the total population of the country. The economy of this region is generally characterized by low per capita income, inadequate infrastructure, geographical isolation, inadequate exploitation of natural resources like minerals, hydropower and forests, low industrialization and high unemployment among the relatively literate people. Owing to its geographical location and proximity to neighboring countries the Northeast region has a natural trading advantage. Border trade has a special significance to the economies of the northeastern states due to their peculiar geographical location. These states have a longer border with neighboring countries than with mainland India. With the exception of the tiny "chicken neck" connecting Assam with West Bengal the rest of the border is shared with Bhutan, China, Myanmar and Bangladesh. Due to its isolation and poor infrastructure the region as a whole is looking to the neighboring countries for improved economic relations and development.

Causes for Border Trade

A number of reasons have been put forward by economists to explain the basic causes for trade that flows across the borders:

(a) availability of certain goods in one side of the border and their non-availability in the other side, *a la Kravis* (1956),

(b) comparative advantage in some lines of production enjoyed by one side of the border and the same in other lines by the other side of the border, *a la Ricardo* (1951),

(c) preference similarity, *a la Linder* (1961), among the people across the border particularly when the border cuts across a uniform cultural plane inhabited by a single ethno-cultural community.[1]

Most of the states in the Northeast share a common boundary with Bangladesh. The Northeast region's borders with Bangladesh stretch to about 1940 kilometers. This region shares only 2 percent of its borders with mainland India while it shares 98 percent of its borders with Bhutan, China, Myanmar and Bangladesh. Border trade with Myanmar and Bangladesh assumes significance for the region. As per the 1994 Government of India notification India has a total of 138 authorized land custom stations (hereinafter LCS) along its borders with neighboring countries. Out of these, India has 90 land custom stations with Bangladesh the highest number with any neighboring country. However it does not mean that all the LCS are operational. In 1997 two additional LCS were opened along the Indo-Bhutan border and in 2006 another border trade point was reopened through the Nathu-La Pass in Sikkim. In figures there are altogether 141 LCS along India's borders with its neighboring countries. Although there is no formal trade agreement between India and Bangladesh a large part of formal bilateral trade flows across these borders particularly through the West Bengal-Bangladesh sector. Besides this route considerable trade also flows across the Northeast-Bangladesh sector. Bilateral trade between India and Bangladesh has undoubtedly become important over the past many years. Although Bangladesh is one of India's important trade partners and export destinations, especially for the northeastern region, the immense possibility for further creation of trade between these countries has not yet been translated into reality.

Export-Import Trends: Northeast Region and Bangladesh

Trade between the Northeast and Bangladesh is generally characterized as a growth generating trade. This trade is primarily caused due to availability of certain natural and agro-forests products in the region and their non-availability in Bangladesh. The Northeast region's (hereinafter NER) exports to Bangladesh consist mainly of mineral products like coal and limestone, natural products like boulders and stone chips and a few agro-horticultural products. About 90 percent of the region's exports to Bangladesh consist of mineral products primarily from Meghalaya. There exists a firm base for the NER-Bangladesh trade due to their mutual complementarities. The natural resources of the region are complementary to the demand structure of the Bangladesh economy. The demand for mineral resources by Bangladesh has led to the exploitation of the mineral resources of Meghalaya even before border trade was opened between Bangladesh and Meghalaya. With the opening of trade between NER-Bangladesh through

Meghalaya there has been a commercial exploitation of mineral resources especially deposits of coal estimated to be 563 million tonnes and limestone estimated at 4147 million tonnes. Even boulder stones were extracted and exported to Bangladesh in huge quantities. Trade relationship between India and Bangladesh has a detrimental bilateral relationship. The geographic proximity factor has made Bangladesh one of India's biggest trading partners especially with the Northeast region. Bangladesh has a staggering trade deficit of more than 1 billion US dollars with India. Bangladesh's imports from India figured at 1022 million US dollars in fiscal year 2001-02 while its exports to India were worth only 50.28 million US dollars. On an average Bangladesh's annual imports from Northeast India amount to over one billion US dollars against its average annual exports of 57 million US dollars. Bangladesh is a big market for products of Meghalaya including minerals which form 90% of NER exports to Bangladesh. Other items include saris and electrical items from Assam, handicrafts from Tripura and some items from Mizoram though the bulk of the region's exports are from Meghalaya. With the approval of the central government the Assam government has recently exported bamboo to Bangladesh on a large scale. In an address at a seminar on "Land Custom Stations Infrastructure", Altaf Jalil stated that the objective was to increase trade between Bangladesh and the Northeast as most of the region's revenue comes through trade from this country. To do so one has to identify Non-Trade Barriers (hereinafter NTBs) and study them to see how they can be removed or reduced to facilitate trade.

Trade statistics for import-export between Northeast India and Bangladesh show that a variety of goods and services are imported and exported. The following tables show the export-import trade statistics between Bangladesh and Northeast India for the year 2002-03 and 2003-04 on a survey

TABLE 7.1

Bangladesh–Northeast India's Trade Data* (Import)

Item (Import)	*FY – 2002 - 2003*		*FY – 2003 - 2004*	
	Quantity (MT)	*Value (000' US$)*	*Quantity (MT)*	*Value (000' US$)*
Coal	710519.4	29617.12	656248.83	27173.47
Boulder Stone	12000.0	6.24	700.00	3.60
Naspati- Pear	43.9	4.56	15.20	1.57
Ginger	217.3	53.39	108.19	22.48
Orange	133.1	30.39	826.60	176.21
Shatkora	27.9	5.93	36.01	6.77
Chilli	2.9	2.08	4.47	3.89
Betel Leaf	1.9	1.85	3.30	2.90
Latex	81.0	52.55	nil	nil
Vegetable	1.1	0.49	nil	nil
Salted Fish	4.0	2.77	nil	nil
Coriander Seeds	59.0	12.27	nil	nil
Sugar	0.5	0.74	nil	nil
Rubber Sheet	8.0	6.95	nil	nil
LPG &LNG bulbs	0.13	14.18	nil	nil
Plastic covers of Motor Cycles	10 pieces	0.02	nil	nil
Aluminum Tiffin Carriers	2 pieces	0.01	nil	nil
Kitchen Utensils	1000 pieces	0.01	nil	nil
Shoes	16 pieces	0.06	nil	nil
Plastic Items	33 pieces	0.03	nil	nil
Men's Garments	144 pieces	0.23	nil	nil
Saris	7 pieces	0.02	nil	nil
Screws	2 sets	0.02	nil	nil
Misc. Baggage	nil	nil	NA	0.65
Dry Fish	nil	nil	105.50	10.95
Natural Rubber	nil	nil	15.96	14.05
Limestone	nil	nil	400.00	2.81
Potato Seeds	nil	nil	80.00	10.73
Fresh Tomatoes	nil	nil	4.00	1.24
Sanitary Items	nil	nil	208 pieces	1.70

Note: NA – Not available, MT – Metric Tonne.

* This table is based on data collected from Tamabil, Dawki, Sheola, Sutarkhandi, Juri-Batuli, Old Ragnabazar, Akhaura, Agartala, Bibirbazar, Srimantapur Land Custom Stations.

collected by the Bangladesh Export Import (hereinafter BEI) team from the various land custom stations located along the border. This is the latest survey conducted by any team about the export-import trade statistics.

Table 7.1 shows the Bangladesh-Northeast India trade data in imports. The bulk of this trade includes coal and boulder stones which are being exported in large quantities. However the amount exported decreased in the financial year 2003-04. Coal exports in 2002-03 were 710519.4 metric tonnes but in the year 2003-04 they came down to 656248.83 metric tonnes. The same trend was witnessed in the case of boulder stones. The export of these mineral resources forms the bulk of revenue for the region in particular and the country in general. Apart from these mineral resources agro-horticultural products are also exported from Meghalaya. These items include oranges, ginger, chilli and betel leaf which have shown an increase. Legitimate trade from Assam and other northeastern states include handloom textiles, stainless steel, utensils, automotive parts, cycle parts and pharmaceutical products. Though these items were present in small quantities in the year 2002-03 they tend to be negative in 2003-04. It has also been observed that certain products such as limestone and natural rubber which were absent in 2002-03 were exported in 2003-04.

On the other hand the region imports numerous commodities from Bangladesh. Table 7.2 indicates that consumer items like biscuits, wafers, drinks and potato crackers which were imported from Bangladesh have increase from 2002-03 to 2003-04. Other commodities include electrical items and dry fish which however come in small quantities. There exists an imbalance trade relationship between Bangladesh and India. Studies conducted during the past decade indicate that legal imports from India were 32 times greater than Bangladesh's exports to India. Trade

TABLE 7.2

Bangladesh-Northeast India's Trade Data* (Export)

Item (Import)	*FY – 2002 - 2003*		*FY – 2003 - 2004*	
	Quantity (MT)	*Value (000' US$)*	*Quantity (MT)*	*Value (000' US$)*
Biscuits & Wafers	4.8	4.98	4471.962	26.55
Battery Plates	3.0	1.04	24.2	10.14
Drinks & potato crackers	14.68	2.28	NA	19.40
CI Sheets	1.5	1.00	nil	nil
Cotton Saris	150 pieces	0.31	.750	1.55
Plastic Doors	15 pieces	0.31	nil	nil
Mosquito Nets	1200 meters	1.25	NA	11.25
Hilsa Fish	NA	112.49	NA	816.29
Dry Fish	NA	80.07	NA	80.88
Waste Cotton	NA	13.32	NA	21.33
Stone Chips	NA	6.41	NA	109.97
Molasses	NA	1.53	NA	11.21
Carding Machines	NA	0.63	nil	nil
Soap, Powder	nil	nil	33.3	47.47
Juice Products	nil	nil	NA	625.53
Charger Lights	nil	nil	6000 pieces	0.24
Ceramic Tiles	nil	nil	NA	3.67
Lay Flat Tubes	nil	nil	NA	126.00
Tin foils	nil	nil	.5	0.33
Foam	nil	nil	260 pieces	0.35
Miscellaneous	nil	nil	NA	558.81

Note: NA – Not available, MT – Metric Tonne.

* This table is based on data collected from Tamabil, Dawki, Sheola, Sutarkhandi, Juri-Batuli, Old Ragnabazar, Akhaura, Agartala, Bibirbazar, Srimantapur Land Custom Stations.

takes place through all the land custom stations situated at various places along the Northeast region-Bangladesh border. Two-way trade between Bangladesh and Northeast India takes place through the following points:

Karimganj-Jokiganj Ferryhat (Assam- Bangladesh border)
Sutarkhandi-Sheola (Assam-Bangladesh border)
Srimantapur-Bibirbazar (Tripura-Bangladesh border)
Dawki-Tamabil (Meghalaya-Bangladesh border)

Since the Northeast has large volumes of resource based exportable products which require large carrying costs it makes sense to have good land custom stations and roads near the source of raw materials. Trade between the Northeast and Bangladesh could be enhanced with the development of infrastructure and better trade agreements between India and Bangladesh. In examining Table 7.1 it has been observed that trade between the two countries has been decreasing. This may be due to certain factors which if discovered could remove the hindrances to trade and bring in more revenue to the state exchequers of both countries.

Informal Trade—Its Causes and Impact

While considering the prospects of regional and sub-regional economic cooperation in South Asia it is important to define and analyze any impediments to such cooperation. The greatest impediment is the existence of informal trade between neighboring countries. Informal trade is characterized by unrecorded transactions, non-payment of taxes, the use of illegal channels, the evasion of duties and a complex system of finance that is not organized but is only an exchange of goods between people in border areas who evade proper channels. Studies reveal the fact that at least 50% of trade with the eastern side of the sub-continent flows through informal channels. It is an established fact that not only is informal trade flourishing in the region but it is also being sustained. This indicates that the economic actors who are responsible for the existence and functioning of the informal sectors are well organized and have well established ties with local border authorities whose main concern is stopping illegal trade. Even though the Border Security Force (hereinafter BSF), the state police along with the Bangladesh Rifles (hereinafter BDR) are entrusted with responsibility of ensuring security along the international border with the power to arrest, no raids have been conducted to contain informal trade. Even along the Meghalaya-Bangladesh international border much of the trade that is being carried out is informal. The informal economy has just the opposite characteristics of a formal economy. Transactions within the informal sector are not governed by well-established rules and regulations and therefore informal transactions are not recorded and are not accounted for when calculating the gross domestic product. Informal transactions are characterized by lack of transparency and restricted market information. It is inconclusive to state that formal trade barriers (such as tariffs) motivate economic actors to turn to the informal trade, there may be non-economic reasons of doing so. Historically, Bangladesh had adopted restrictive trade policies while tariff and non-tariff barriers restricted the flow of imports into the domestic market. Unfortunately, such restrictive policies persuade certain economic actors to engage in illegal trade which hindered the government's efforts to collect revenue and to initiate measures to protect the domestic market. Studies conducted throughout Bangladesh and the Northeast India indicate that smugglers try to maximize their profits by smuggling commodities to a high price destination while simultaneously evading taxes. Profits are not only distributed amongst the smugglers but are also shared amongst all "stakeholders" such as law enforcement and border authorities, whose cooperation is imperative to the smugglers activities. Thus restrictive policies on trade ensure high price differentials which in turn attract illegal traders to engage in illegal trade and also enhance the profit incentive of smugglers.

Bilateral trade between India and Bangladesh has undoubtedly become important over the past few years. This trade is however marked by an imbalance. India's exports to Bangladesh are greater than its imports from Bangladesh. The deficit incurred by Bangladesh on both the formal and informal frontiers poses a problem and so it is vital for both governments to implement measures to curb the informal trade that exists. Strict observation of rules, regulations and procedures are needed along the Bangladesh-Northeast India international border. The quantum of illegal trade between Meghalaya's border villages with Bangladesh alone is around the same as the amount of formal trade. The informal trade – a euphemism for smuggling – is estimated to be worth Rs 200 crores annually according to former Chief Secretary of Meghalaya S.K.Tiwari. This he said happens to be the same as the formal trade amount. In an interview with the *Indian Express* he observed that the total amount of trade both legal and illegal is around 400 crores which is huge compared to the amount of formal trade which comes to around Rs 170-200 crores annually which is being carried out by surveys.

Barun Harun Ur Rashid former Bangladesh ambassador to the United Nations General Assembly stated that whatever occurs in the Northeast states of India has a direct and visible impact on Bangladesh since it is almost an "India locked" country. Though the potential for growth in trade between the Northeast and Bangladesh exists the high incidence of informal trade between India and Bangladesh continues to be a concern for trade and industry. According to the Federation of Indian Chamber of Commerce and Industry (hereinafter FICCI) informal trade between the two countries in commodities include food items and live animals apart from consumer goods. Commodities unofficially imported from Bangladesh are confined to a small band of items including fabrics and spices. If informal trade still increases it would lead to a loss of revenue for the states in the region. The volume of unofficial export to Bangladesh is reported to be in the range of 350-500 million dollars (US) per year.

Potential of Northeast-Bangladesh Trade

It is possible to chalk out a trade plan for the Northeast and Bangladesh. Both want to maximize their respective national interests and to develop the border areas where the task to enhance trade is easier through cross border cooperation than through national efforts alone. It is important to realize the potential of border trade on the basis of the pattern of exchange taking place across the border while also taking into account the volume of cross-border informal trade. Delivering a paper at a seminar at the Bangladesh Enterprise Institute on May 31, 2005, Rajiv Sikri, Secretary (East), Ministry of External Affairs, Government of India spoke of the trade relations between India and Bangladesh. He stated that India and Bangladesh have great potential for trade relations irrespective of the trade deficits. However the amount of informal trade going on is a great hindrance for increasing formal trade. This is of great concern as the potential of NER-Bangladesh trade is relatively large. Sikri also stated that Bangladesh was very special to India. It is India's largest neighbor with the largest regular trade relations. He went on to say that India recognized Bangladesh's importance in the Northeast region because it controls the rest of India's access to the Northeast.

The resource structure of the northeast region is complementary to the demand structure of Bangladesh. There exists a firm base for NER-Bangladesh trade in their mutual complementarities. What we observe in the NER-Bangladesh border trade is that it has accelerated the exploration of local resources even though it has established only a dyadic linkage between trade and resource use. A triadic linkage for up gradation of production structure is observed only in cement production. The number of cement producing units in Meghalaya have increased from one to six within the last thirty years. In this era of economic globalization and stiff competition almost all researchers working on Indo-Bangladesh cooperation have indicated that a closer cooperation or integration of Bangladesh's economy with that of the Northeastern states will turn the eastern region into a hub of economic activity. The neglected Northeastern region has the potential to become an engine of economic growth.

Problems of Border Trade

In the long term there may be difficulties in the export and import of goods due to numerous bottlenecks leading the people of both countries to resort to smuggling rather than formal trade. Border trade could definitely boost the economy of the region but if the problems are not addressed trade will not increase. First, the unnatural borders created by the British through the partition of Bengal in 1905 is responsible for the geographical isolation of the Northeast from the rest of India except for the 22 kilometers "chicken neck" connecting Assam with West Bengal. Second, after the emergence of Bangladesh in 1971 both countries concluded the 1974 Mujib-Indira Agreement on the demarcation of Bangladesh-India land boundary. The purpose was to accurately define certain points and to complete the demarcation of the land boundary between India and Bangladesh. Regrettably for more than thirty years India has failed to rectify the agreement and as a result a 6.5 km long boundary on the east involving one of the northeastern states remains undemarcated. Third, security concerns and misunderstanding are also another reason which poses as a bottleneck to enhanced trade. Insurgency in the states of the Northeast has a destabilizing impact on the tribal belt of Bangladesh. Misunderstanding between the two countries regarding insurgency has led the two countries to drift further apart with India repeatedly alleging that Bangladesh has done nothing to drive out the militant groups of northeast India entrenched in Bangladesh territory. This has created a mistrust bringing their relationship to the lowest possible ebb in recent times. The misunderstanding has adversely affected the overall bilateral relationship.

As stated earlier the amount of informal trade being carried out is also one of the biggest hurdles in increasing economic cooperation between the two countries. Sikri notes that economic relationships are very complex and cannot be seen only from a purely trade basis. An enormous amount of smuggling is being carried out and India is also losing foreign exchange earnings. Unless there is wholehearted cooperation both sides stand to lose. With regard to Meghalaya mistrust between the people on both sides of the border is also another problem. On many occasions it has been observed especially in the border areas that people from the other side of the border enter Meghalaya carry away goods with such ease even though the Border Security Force and the Bangladesh Rifles are patrolling the international border. The BSF, the BDR and the state police are central to any effort to contain the flow of illegal goods. Not only in Meghalaya but also in other states such as Assam and Tripura illegal trade continues under the watchful eyes of these security agencies. Such incidents will tend to create mistrust among people of both countries. Fencing the border along the no man's land is not permissible under the Bangladesh-India Border Guidelines according to Bangladesh authorities as it is offensive to the people of Bangladesh. India however does not understand Bangladesh's interpretation of the word "defense" structure in the guidelines. One reality is that political and economic relations are intertwined and cannot be separated. As such people of both countries face such a stand-off. If such problems cannot be addressed then trade will not prosper. What is required is that the pending issues need to be spelt out clearly and discussed between the two countries. The late B.B. Lyngdoh, former Chief Minister of Meghalaya had sent several requests to the Union Government for opening of border *haats* as was done before the partition. This initiative would bring revenue to the State of Meghalaya and also cut down the amount of informal trade. However nothing has been done even by the present Meghalaya Democratic Alliance (hereinafter MDA) government to sort out this issue. If the government does not realize the gravity of the problem then trade will always tend to be informal. Clashes between the security forces on both sides of the border have further escalated mistrust among the two countries. The first incident occurred on April 15, 2005 when the BDR occupied Pyrdiwah, a village located in Meghalaya and the second incident occurred on April 18, 2005 in Boraibari in the Assam-Bangladesh border where fifteen BSF personnel were shot dead by the BDR on the claim that the former intruded into Bangladesh territory. As long as these contentious issues remain unattended and differences are not ironed out in a way that satisfies the common people on both sides of an arbitrarily carved out border, they will further lead to futile clashes between the soldiers of both these countries who are required to defend a 4000 kilometer border parts of which keeps on changing due to the unpredictable course of rivers that run from India into Bangladesh and also due to undemarcated stretches such as the 6.5 km stretch that has not yet been marked out. In order to address these problems the governments of both countries should have sustained and regular discussions to create conditions for a win-win situation.

Suggestive Measures

Certain measures to enhance trade prospects between the Northeast and Bangladesh can be suggested:

(a) Both Bangladesh and the northeastern states possess vast energy resources including gas, coal, forests and potential hydel power. The region's acute energy shortage has been a major reason for its poor economic growth. If economic integration or cooperation between Bangladesh and the northeastern states is evolved both Bangladesh and India will reap immense benefits.

(b) Better road connectivity and infrastructure is a necessity for improving trade relations. This suggestion was mooted by Donkupar Roy who represents the border constituency of Shella. Speaking to the *Shillong Times* Roy noted that if the Nathu-La Pass could be reopened with so much investment there is also a similar need to open trade routes from Meghalaya to Bangladesh. Before initiating trade border roads need improvement for better connectivity, rail links could also be revived to facilitate trade relations with Bangladesh. Bangladesh is a big market for the local products of Meghalaya. The Chattak industrial area in Bangladesh is only about five to six kilometers away from the Meghalaya border. He also noted that the Government of Meghalaya has stressed on the fact that the centre should take up the issue of improved economic ties between India and Bangladesh beyond the political relations.

(c) Opening of border *haats* is another option which the central government as well as the state governments of the Northeast should consider as an alternative to improve trade. Considering the potential of border trade with Bangladesh as was reflected in the 11th Five Year Plan meet, the former Chief Minister of Meghalaya J.D. Rymbai emphasized the need for having trade ties with Bangladesh. He is of the view that border *haats* should be reopened as they would boost the economy of the villages located along the international border.

(d) Setting up of industries along the border may also be

advantageous as it can prove to be cost-effective. This may take the form of branching out or collaborative ventures with the local or regional businesses. The central government may establish free trade zones along the international border and encourage the setting up of export processing zones in the border towns.

(e) Bangladesh and India need to cooperate at unprecedented levels given their economic potential. As India continues to expand Bangladesh can utilize this opportunity by marketing its goods in India thereby creating a market for Bangladeshi goods in a growing Indian economy. In order to ensure this both countries need to address the issues of tariff and non-tariff barriers which perpetuate illegal trade. The role of the government is essential in dictating the behavior of these economic actors.

(f) At a recent meeting in New Delhi on export possibilities with Bangladesh, the former Chief Secretary of Meghalaya S.K. Tiwari stated that proper banking facilities at LCS in the border areas is a necessity for quick transaction and to prevent informal trade in the region. He noted that horticultural products from Meghalaya could be exported to Bangladesh as there was high demand for them. (Similar thoughts were echoed by Jairam Ramesh when he addressed the National Seminar at Synod College). At the same meeting Tiwari also suggested that the Commerce Ministry could consider a transport subsidy on air freight charges at the rate of 90% for all items of export through LCS or airports.

(g) Bangladesh and the northeastern states could reap huge benefits if they only realize that they are in a win-win situation. Creating a bigger market for Bangladeshi goods can earn huge revenue for the region. Both countries can earn substantial revenue if Indian goods are allowed to pass through Bangladesh territory or through the Chittagong port to the northeastern states to the rest of India. India will in turn save million of dollars in sending goods to the northeastern states through Bangladesh.

(h) Indian industrialists could set up industries in Bangladesh and use its territory to export natural gas to northeastern states.

(i) A package has already been announced by the Commerce Ministry, Government of India for the large scale export of bamboo from Assam to Bangladesh. The government has to ensure that trade does not become informal.

Thus the Northeastern region-Bangladesh border trade has great potential as it can boost the economy of the region as a whole and pave the way for economic integration.

Conclusion

Economic integration has multiplier effects. India and Bangladesh are integrating into a global economy and both cannot escape economic growth and development. Both India and Bangladesh need to address their problems to strengthen economic ties between the two countries. Both countries need to engage in confidence building measures. Border trade will result in increased economic growth in the region. This will help to eradicate poverty, unrest and insurgency in the northeastern states. Economic cooperation will usher in a robust economic growth in Bangladesh and will certainly provide potential and economic dividends to India as well.

REFERENCES

1. Das, Gurudas: "Border Trade in India's North-East: Theory and Practice" in David R. Syiemlieh et al. *Challenges of Development in North-East India: Theory and Practice*, Regency Publications, New Delhi, 2006.

Sources Cited

1. *Administrator*, "Border Trade: Need to Tap Growth Potential"
2. Cookson, Forrest E. and Shamsul, A.K.M. Alan (ed.): *Towards Greater Sub-Regional Economic Cooperation*, The University Press Limited, 2002.
3. Jalil, Altaf : "Land Custom Stations Infrastructure", paper presented at Seminar held at BEI on March 22, 2005. http:/www.bei.bd.org/newslett/nei/0305/art3.htm
4. Mishra, Richa: "Indo-Bangla informal trade cause for concern: FICCI" *The Hindu Business Line*, November 11, 2004.
5. *The Indian Express*, January 11, 2006.
6. *The Shillong Times*, July 10, 2006.

8

LOOK EAST POLICY: MEGHALAYA'S COAL TRADE WITH BANGLADESH

Lambodar Rout

This paper is an attempt to present a vivid account of the existing trends in the export of coal from Meghalaya to Bangladesh and its prospects in the context of the Look East Policy. Meghalaya's trade relations with Bangladesh are very old. Most of the British writers have noted this trade relation. Hunter in his account observed that the external commerce of the Khasi and Jaintia Hills is chiefly conducted on the southern boundary through the district of Sylhet.[1] The beginning of the coal trade of Meghalaya with Bangladesh can be traced back to 1842 when Colonel Lister excavated and dispatched 44350 marinds of coal to Chattak.[2] The coal trade could not be sustained due to absence of cost effectiveness in carriage. Oldham made an observation that the extensive districts of Sylhet, Cachar and Munnipore cannot be deprived much longer of the benefit of the Cherrapunjee coal and that of the frontier when communication system will develop. Today we see that his anticipation has come true.

The emergence of Bangladesh as an independent country on December 16th, 1971 is a landmark which introduced a bar-marching character in the trade relations with Northeast India in general and Meghalaya in particular.[3] Meghalaya and Bangladesh share a common border covering a distance of about 423 kilometers. This long border makes Meghalaya a natural trading partner of Bangladesh. Trade with Bangladesh is carried out as per the Indo-Bangladesh Trade Agreement which provides for the "most favored nation" treatment accorded to goods and services traded with Bangladesh. There is an Indo-Bangladesh joint economic commission which meets once a year to discuss outstanding issues pertaining to trade and investment.[4]

Coal Export to Bangladesh from Meghalaya: Its Present Context

Coal export to Bangladesh from Meghalaya started only recently when the Mineral and Metal Trading Corporation of India (hereinafter MMTC) exported about 3000 tonnes of coal in 1987-88. Seeing that the coal requirement of Bangladesh brick kilns was almost 1,00,000 tonnes per annum, the State Government of Meghalaya obtained a special permission from the Government of India in 1989-90 authorizing the export of Meghalaya coal to Bangladesh by the state owned Meghalaya Mineral Development Corporation Ltd (hereinafter MMDC). The MMDC functioned as the commission agent, the mining and supply of coal to the export outlets was carried out by private parties. The Corporation processed the export documents and collected bills from importers in Bangladesh. In lieu of this service the Corporation got a commission from the exporters.[5] In 1989 John Deng Pohrmen was Minister in charge of Mineral Resources, Government of Meghalaya. Though Meghalaya traders started exporting coal to Bangladesh they faced numerous inconveniences as they had to go to Kolkata for clearing transit papers which was an expensive exercise. Pohrmen went to Delhi, met the central minister in charge of mineral resources and persuaded him to delegate the powers of clearance to the custom office at Dawki. This was done to the immense benefit of the coal traders. On his initiative custom offices were subsequently opened at Borsora in West Khasi Hills and Ghasuapara in South Garo Hills. Coal became the "black gold" in Meghalaya. By easing the coal exporting facilities to Bangladesh many traders had become multi-millionaires. With the passage of time coal trade with Bangladesh was carried out by an umbrella organization of all international traders, the Meghalaya International Traders Association (hereinafter MITA).

Export Procedures

Coal to Bangladesh is carried out by international exporters. These exporters employ one manager and one assistant to look after export activities. Information gathered from the field reveals that each international exporter spends Rs.15,000-20,000/- to run their office. First a letter of credit is collected from international importers which state the demand for coal export. This letter of credit is produced before the Directorate of Mineral Resources, (hereinafter DMR) Government of Meghalaya and a challan is obtained for the coal to be exported by paying a fee of Rs.165/- per tonne. Then the Meghalaya International Exporters Chamber of Commerce issues a per shipment certificate of origin on behalf of the Superintendence Company of India Private Limited, recognized by the Ministry of Commerce, Government of India by charging a fee of Rs. 3/- per tonne. After completing all these formalities and obtaining the necessary documents coal is then exported to Bangladesh.

Coal Trade with Bangladesh from Border Points

Trade with Bangladesh takes place from the following border points of Meghalaya: Baghmara of South Garo Hills; Dalu, Ghasuapara, Mahendraganj of West Garo Hills; Bholaganj, Balat, Shella Bazar, Ryngu of East Khasi Hills; Borsora of West Khasi Hills and Dawki of Jaintia Hills. In

TABLE 8.1

Meghalaya's Coal Export to Bangladesh Through Different LCS *(Quantity in Metric Tonnes)*

Name of LCS	1998-99	1999-00	2000-01	2001-02	2002-03	2003-04	2004-05
Dawki	61.94	34.01	51.43	43.32	47.32	39.13	22.49
	341862.121	222426.457	420622.418	304061.751	494966.534	478056	311329
Borsora	12.64	25.51	28.58	24.1	23.19	30.49	29.7
	69793.200	166804.735	233758.200	169211.83	242577.50	372466.7	411328
Mahendraganj	0	9.37	2.09	0	2.24	1.94	0.2
	0	61290.47	17133	0	23515	23743.5	2858
Ghasuapara	10.27	14.16	15.82	17.46	10.42	6.39	6.7
	56684.5	92597.9	129386.2	122577.1	109012.406	78059.6	92852.4
Dalu	0.15	0.15	0.62	0.58	1.39	1.14	2.56
	861	1007.5	5087	4089.7	14548.8	13927.1	35529
Baghmara	0	0	0	0.014	0.023	0.2	0
	0	0	0	100	250	350	0
Karimganj	0	0	0	1.43	1.26	1.2	0
	0	0	11740	8851.76	12594	2462.3	0
Sutarkhandi	14.97	30.94	9.66	13.24	14.19	20.67	38.31
	82655.364	202328.206	79057.323	92953.785	148441.165	252502.3	530374.2
Total	551856.185	746455.268	896784.141	701845.926	1045905.405	1221567.5	1384270.6

Source: Custom Office, Shillong and DMR, Government of Meghalaya.

the case of Assam it takes place along the following points Karimganj, Steamerghat and Sutarkhandi. In the case of Tripura coal is exported along Mannu, Agartala and Srimantapura. At present Meghalaya coal is exported to Bangladesh through some land custom stations located both in Meghalaya and Assam. There are six land customs stations namely Dawki, Borsora, Mahendraganj, Ghasuapara, Dalu and Baghmara in Meghalaya and two LCS, Karimganj and Sutarkhandi in Assam from where Meghalaya coal is exported to Bangladesh. The Table 8.1 illustrates the amount of coal which is exported to Bangladesh through different land customs stations in different years.

From the analysis of data in the Table 8.1 it is evident that there are three important land customs stations located in Meghalaya through which coal is significantly exported to Bangladesh. Dawki LCS occupies the first position except for the year 2004-2005. Borsora occupies the second place while and Ghasuapara stands third in terms of total volume of coal exports to Bangladesh. In the case of Assam, Sutarkhandi LCS is an important point from where a significant amount of Meghalaya coal is exported. In 2004-05, 38.31% of total coal export went through this land custom station. A close perusal at the data reveals the fact that there has been a continuous upward trend in the total amount of coal being exported to Bangladesh. In 1998-99, the total amount of coal exported was 551856.185 mt which went up to 1384270.6 mt in 2004-05.

Having seen the composition pattern of coal export a comparable analysis of the total coal exported to Bangladesh is made with the total coal extracted in Meghalaya through the following Table 8.2.

TABLE 8.2

Total Coal Exported to Bangladesh as Percentage to Total Coal Production in Meghalaya *(Quantity in '000 Tonnes)*

Year	*Total Coal Export to Bangladesh*	*Total Coal Production in Meghalaya*	*Percentage of Coal Export to Total Production*
1998-99	551.856	4237.06	13.02
1999-00	746.455	4060.10	18.38
2000-01	896.784	4064.90	22.06
2001-02	701.845	5149.30	13.62
2002-03	1045.905	4396.20	23.79
2003-04	1221.567	5439.10	22.45
2004-05	1384.270	5525.20	25.05

Source: Custom Office Shillong and DMR, Government of Meghalaya.

From the above table it is clear that coal export performance is showing a steady growth over the years. In 1998-99 coal export to Bangladesh from Meghalaya was 13.02% of the total coal extracted while in 2004-05 it was 25.05%, so there is a potential coal market in Bangladesh for Meghalaya coal. As mentioned the Bangladesh brick manufacturing units depend upon Meghalaya's coal. In addition coal is also required for the Chattak Cement factory. The demand for coal in Bangladesh is always greater than the supply. Hence there is a scope for Meghalaya to increase its coal export to Bangladesh.[6]

Trade Facilitation Bottlenecks along Indo-Bangladesh Border—A Case Study of Dawki Land Customs Station

A. Lack of proper trade facilities is a major concern in most of the Indo-Bangladesh land custom stations. To take a stock of all these trade facilitation bottlenecks a case study of Dawki land custom station was carried out. The following problems were found:

(a) The parking lots at Dawki lack even basic amenities such as drinking water and public utilities. The approach road to the LCS is very congested, there is no government bonded warehouse to provide storage services in this town.

(b) Dawki is located about 55 kilometers from Jowai, the district head quarters of Jaintia Hills. The coal that is traded through Dawki originates mainly from the following places: Bapung, Rymbai, Ladrymbai, Kongong, Lyngkhat, Sutnga, Skhentalang, Jarain and they are carried to the Dawki border by trucks through the National Highway 40E formally known as Jowai-Dawki road. The delay in transportation of coal is a normal phenomenon due to (i) Border Security Force restrictions (ii) time consuming documentation process at the custom office (iii) DMR measurement of coal laden trucks where an average of 400 trucks travel daily.

(c) The average transportation cost per km turns out to be very expensive compared to other national highways.

(d) Merchandise has to face substantial loss of time at the border. The delay takes place at the parking lot, in custom clearance and at the entry and exit points. It is mandatory for the trucks coming from Bapung, Ladrymbai and other areas to park at Amtapoh just after the Amlarem sub-division, Jaintia Hills District. The trucks are allowed to move serially towards Dawki when maximum trucks are cleared from the LCS point. At the border, the trucks are again made to park at the parking space. After getting the clearance from both the DMR and the Indian customs authority trucks can cross the border between 10:00A.M. – 5.30P.M.

(e) The existing custom clearance procedures at the border lead to significant costs and delay. The existing custom procedures and documentation are not transparent. As a result, all the exporters employ clearing agents on a monthly basis. In spite of appointing clearing agents and paying "speed money" to the custom and DMR officials, clearance of papers requires much more time than it should according to the exporters.

(f) The entry points at the border have one single gate which is used for exports, imports as well as for passenger movement. At a time only one truck can pass through the gate. As a result the entry point remains very congested.

(g) The Indian trucks after unloading at Tamabil (in Bangladesh) are allowed to re-enter India before or after export hours. They have to park along the road side in Muktapur which is located ahead of Dawki LCS.

B. Transaction Cost

Transaction cost has become one of the important issues for traders in most of the underdeveloped countries of the world. In a recent issue the World Bank Development Report states that corruption increases the transaction cost.[7] A similar situation is faced by our traders in Meghalaya. For formal traders transaction costs include bribes paid at various stages to officials over and above standard expenses which include insurance and cost of credit. The additional transaction costs incurred by the Indian exporters who are engaged in trade with Bangladesh include speed money and delays.

C. Informal Trade

The informal component of border trade between India and Bangladesh is substantial. Informal or illegal trade takes place not only through legal and conventional routes but through other routes which subsequently escape the notice of the BSF and customs personnel. It is said that illegal imports and exports are as large as their formal counterpart.[8]

TABLE 8.3

Seizure Cases in Indo-Bangladesh Trade: Figure of Northest Region

Year	*Case*	*Value (Lakhs)*
2000-01	6828	528.17
2001-02	7274	892.18
2002-03	7405	969.83
2003-04	7687	581.90
2004-05	7789	813.27

Source: Custom Office, Shillong.

From the Table 8.3 we find that total number of seizure cases during last five years is 36983 and the total value of seized goods works out to be 37.85 crores. The possible reason behind this higher value may be because certain very high valued goods are either smuggled in or out through the northeastern international borders. It is relevant to know the main items of smuggled goods across the Indo-Bangladesh border in the Khasi and Jaintia Hills of Meghalaya. A close look at the smuggled items across the Indo-Bangladesh border makes it evident that the goods smuggled included high value materials like gold, prohibited articles like narcotics, drugs, liquor and ganja. The reasons for this may be due to the prohibitive tariff, non-tariff barriers like high cost of documentation, wide variation in the method of assessment of duties and failure of SAPTA negotiations. In addition to these factors lack of adequate physical infrastructure at the border check-posts and lack of transit rights also account for the indulgence in smuggling across the border.[9]

TABLE 8.4

Main Items Smuggled Across Indo-Bangladesh-Shillong Sector (Khasi and Jaintia Hills of Meghalaya)

Items illegally exported	*Items illegally imported*
Bidi	Gold
Sugar	Currency
Motor parts	Pirated CDs
Betel Leaves and Betel Nut	Audio Cassettes
Ganja	Cheap cosmetics
Phensidyl	Cigarettes
Liquor	Potato Chips
Timber	Dry fish
Boulder stone	

Source: Custom Office, Shillong.

Conclusion

Union Minister of State for Commerce, Jairam Ramesh in his recent visit to Dawki has asked the state government of Meghalaya to commence construction work of the proposed Dawki dry port which has so far been a non starter mired in disputes. This proposed project is to commence on the portion of land where there are no disputes or legal hurdles. The Central Warehousing Corporation (hereinafter CWC) will be the implementing agency for the dry port estimated to cost twenty crores. This port will be equipped with all the modern facilities to ensure the smooth export of coal and other commodities to Bangladesh. In addition Ramesh also launched BSNL's CellOne service at Dawki to bring the areas along the international border under mobile phone network. This is the first cell phone facility of its kind to be launched in border areas and will go a long way to facilitate trade and connectivity.[10]

Keeping in view all the problems discussed it may be concluded that if the "Look East Policy" is implemented with the view to improve physical infrastructure in land customs stations, to lessen the documentation procedures and to improve diplomatic relations, the coal trade as well as other formal trade can be enhanced significantly to the benefit of the people of Meghalaya.

REFERENCES

1. Hunter, W.W.: *A Statistical Account of Assam*, Vol. 2, Reprint 1998.
2. Oldham, Thomas: *Geology, Meteorology and Economy of Meghalaya*, Mittal Publications, New Delhi, 1984.
3. Madan, D.K.: *Indo-Bangladesh Economic relations and SAARC*, Deep and Deep Publications, New Delhi,1996.
4. Agnihotri, S.K.: "Border trade with Bangladesh", *Journal of NEICSSR*, Vol. 11, no. 2, October, 1993.
5. Agnihotri, S.K.: *op.cit.*
6. *The Shillong Times*, March 20, 2003.
7. *Bangladesh: Growth and Export Competitiveness*, World Bank Report No. 31394 BD, 2005
8. Rahman, Atier: "Bangladesh-India Economic Relations: Potentials and Imperatives", *Artha Beekshan*, Journal of Bangiya Arthaniti Parishad (Bengal Economic Association) Vol. 13, No. 3, December 2004.
9. Rahman, Atier: *op.cit.*
10. The *Shillong Times*, September 25, 2007.

9

REGIONAL ECONOMIC COOPERATION BETWEEN INDIA AND ASEAN: TRADE OPPORTUNITIES FOR THE NORTHEAST REGION

Ratul Mahanta & Daisy Das

Introduction

Regional economic cooperation has become necessary in the post-World War II era as is evident from the success of the European Union and ASEAN. Not only developing countries but even the most developed countries of the world are seen entering into different agreements (such as the European Union, North Atlantic Free Trade Agreement, Latin America Free Trade Agreement) with their neighbors for economic cooperation and to reduce the volume of pressure that arises out of an unprecedented uncertainty emerging in the new international economic order. Such a concept has made its way into India as well. The Look East Policy has opened the door for the first time since Independence to economically link India on a larger scale with its international neighbors. The policy has allowed India to break the artificial political barriers that have severely limited India's ground strategic options in its engagement with Southeast Asia.

Southeast Asia has abundant deposits of mineral

resources, it has a huge prospective to promote tourism which alternatively combines with a host of other resources such as human capital, natural, cultural and ethnic beauty, heritage sites, beaches and deep forests. Despite such resourcefulness, this entire zone has not developed up to the potential that it can. The per capita income of the constituents of this zone is extremely low when compared with the per capita income of that of the USA and European countries. One of the ways of removing the existing poor level of development of this zone is regional cooperation among the units through bilateral trade. In spite of being contiguously located to each other trade among these countries takes place mainly through sea routes. Therefore the volume of existing trade between India and ASEAN countries is lower in comparison to their respective trade relations with European countries and America which are geographically far away from the region. Northeast India though landlocked is ideally positioned both in the geographical and commercial sense, to build the bridge between India and ASEAN. This hardly needs any elaboration. It is no exaggeration to say that besides being a land bridge the Northeast also provides the cultural bridge between India and ASEAN. Due to various reasons though mainly political this bridge could not be activated and utilized over the last few decades for mutual benefit. The end of the cold war lead to a thaw in bilateral relations between ideologically opposed neighbors. Recent developments such as the Indo-Singapore CECA, Indo-Thai FTA, Indo-Malaysia Agreements, BIMST-EC FTA and also the signing of the agreement on South Asia Free Trade Agreement provide unique opportunities to build a new bridge and a sound basis for a new "Indo-ASEAN partnership for the 21st century". It is against this backdrop that an analysis will be made to understand the trend and composition of trade between India and ASEAN and to examine the opportunities to enhance economic development of Northeast India from regional cooperation through border trade with Southeast Asia.

Trade with ASEAN

India is linked with ASEAN through its international border with Myanmar which is spread across several Northeast states. Table 9.1 represents the percentage change of the value of each product of India's export to ASEAN during 1997-98 and 2002-03. It is evident from the table that the percentage change in the export of all commodities from India to ASEAN has increased especially after 1998-99. In 2003-04 out of all exportable commodities, oil meals have shown a positive increase by 161.80 percentages followed by dyes and intermediate goods and primary and semi-finished iron and steel. However during the same year gems and jewellery show a negative change by 22.02.

TABLE 9.1

Percentage Change in the Composition of India's Export to ASEAN during 1997-98 and 2003-04 *(US$ Million)*[1]

Commodity/Year	1997-1998	1998-1999	1999-2000	2000-2001	2001-2002	2002-2003	2003-2004
All commodities	-14.82	-34.15	37.16	28.86	20.44	33.49	25.33
1. Gems and jewellery	-36.32	-0.71	62.92	7.94	15.31	36.98	-22.02
2. Primary & semi finish iron & steel	-6.53	-66.44	58.46	19.76	17.97	79.75	74.68
3. Oil meals	-25.86	-50.42	-8.44	38.43	19.20	-56.15	161.80
4. Electronic goods	-16.40	-35.70	44.38	93.45	20.78	-37.97	26.32
5. Drugs,pharm and fine chemicals	-3.83	14.92	26.13	-3.43	-0.11	20.15	13.92
6. Machinery& instruments	16.52	-39.09	-0.49	16.53	12.84	14.56	3.165
7. Dyes, intermediates etc.	-15.44	-3.56	129.52	-19.24	-21.16	101.84	119.05
8. Manmade yarn fabrics makeup	-36.09	-20.96	65.00	49.94	63.37	31.37	41.18
9. Manufacture of metals	34.36	-38.14	44.62	5.36	2.95	26.63	15.71
10. Agro chemicals	-5.43	-6.39	42 17	36.10	0.57	11.52	17.33
11. Meat & preparations	4.59	-30.35	4.34	64.44	-5.52	1.89	14.80
12. Plastic & linoleum products	-1.08	-3.56	81.67	144.80	11.13	4.90	38.20

Source: Foreign Trade and Balance of Payments, August 2004, CMIE.

Table 9.2 shows the percentage change of India's import from ASEAN during 1997-98 to 2003-04. Except for pulses and manmade filament/spur yarn and waste, all other commodities show a positive percentage change during these years. Looking at the data of the total value of export and import commodities from and to India during these seven years, the balance of trade has been in favor of ASEAN.

TABLE 9.2

Percentage Change in the Composition of India's Import from ASEAN During 1997-1998 and 2003-2004 (US$ Million)[2]

Commodity/Year	1997-1998	1998-1999	1999-2000	2000-2001	2001-2002	2002-2003	2003-2004
All commodities	16.45	19.70	17.88	-20.15	8.30	17.30	42.73
1. Vegetable oils (edible)	-5.57	90.92	7.13	-28.73	-8.83	53.54	52.25
2. Electronic goods	48.87	10.65	47.42	36.78	-10.14	10.45	34.43
3. Woodsand woods products	59.44	-5.04	34.52	-4.79	20.77	-24.08	95.69
4. Organic chemicals	-24.30	-16.34	25.74	24.81	18.09	11.18	57.39
5. Transport equipment	117.11	-26.25	-64.22	43.71	22.04	295.03	85.81
6. Non-electrical machinery	25.87	-11.55	-1.65	55.30	2.54	0.83	5.305
7. Pulses	-1.99	-42.91	-64.53	88.07	422.22	-10.33	-6.85
8. Metal ferrous oils and metal scrap	28.65	66.76	-32.10	-15.43	98.59	7.58	24.50
9. Coal, coke & briquettes	112.63	-2.66	11.78	-2.54	40.95	5.08	45.42
10. Electrical machinery	40.39	16.63	35.49	12.34	-22.80	45.18	38.60
11. Manmade filament/spun yarn/waste	–	–	–	-7.89	39.67	44.53	-23.41
12. Non-ferrous metals	-3.14	-8.34	-16.28	8.68	-15.63	-4.36	40.16

Source: Foreign Trade and Balance of Payments, August 2004, CMIE.

A Comparative Trade Scenario

Table 9.3 and 9.4 show the trend in India's imports from and export to ASEAN and rest of the world. Table 9.3 shows that the proportion of India's export to ASEAN has been increasing over the years. The growth rate of India's export to ASEAN has been growing at the rate of 251 percent.

TABLE 9.3

Export from India to ASEAN and the Rest of the World during 1997-98 to 2003-04 (US$ Million)[3]

Year	*ASEAN*	*Rest of the world*
1997-98	2474.47 (7.06)	35048.67 (100)
1998-98	1629.51 (4.91)	33210.97 (100)
1999-00	2234.99 (6.08)	36759.52 (100)
2000-01	2880.00 (6.52)	44147.44 (100)
2001-02	3468.79 (7.89)	43976.01 (100)
2002-03	4630.53 (8.76)	52856.28 (100)
2003-04	5813.48 (9.14)	63622.50 (100)

Note: Figures in parentheses indicate percentage share of exports from India.

Source: Foreign Trade and Balance of Payments, August 2004, CMIE.

Table 9.4 shows that the proportion of imports from ASEAN to India's total imports had increased to the maximum in 1999-2000, but decreased after that and then again showed an increasing trend which indicated an increasing demand for ASEAN products in the Indian market. The growth rate of imports from ASEAN to India was 210 percent during the period from 1997-98 to 2003-04.

TABLE 9.4

Import to India from ASEAN and the Rest of the World during 1997-98 to 2003-04 (US$ Million)[4]

Year	*ASEAN*	*Rest of the world*
1997-98	3608.11 (8.69)	41534.6 (100)
1998-99	4318.80 (10.19)	42379.20 (100)
1999-00	5090.90 (10.22)	49798.64 (100)
2000-01	4064.88 (8.12)	50056.27 (100)
2001-02	4402.16 (8.53)	51588.41 (100)
2002-03	5163.54 (8.39)	61571.55 (100)
2003-04	7369.78 (9.54)	77236.66 (100)

Note: Figures in parentheses indicate percentage share of exports from India.

Source: Foreign Trade and Balance of Payments, August 2004, CMIE.

Regional Cooperation

The existing value and volume of trade between India and ASEAN shown in the above tables is small if we consider the geographical proximity and huge potential existing. The transportation bottlenecks and the protectionist policy followed in the pre-globalization period can be treated as a major cause for the low volume of trade among these countries. Lack of wider markets has impeded the economic development and the process of exploitation of potentialities of all these countries. However in recent years all the governments in the Northeast region have shown keen interest in removing these bottlenecks by endeavoring to establish regional cooperation. Moreover to compete with the pressure of economic progress experienced by developed countries of the west, it is of paramount importance for India and all Southeast Asian countries to increase economic cooperation between them. The two way level India-ASEAN trade is sought to be raised to US$ 30 billion by 2007, which presently stands only at US$ 12.5 billion. The other long term objectives include –

(a) to build an ASEAN-India Free Trade Area (FTA) in the next ten years

(b) to develop an Asian Economic Community by or before 2020

(c) to eventually create a common currency for Asia.

In this respect the Government of India recently declared the same currency to be used in trade with Myanmar from 2005. To make all these objectives a reality China, Japan, India and South Korea must also join the ten member countries of ASEAN. In 2001, India and Malaysia signed a number of bilateral agreements, a memorandum of understanding and business-to-business agreements thereby laying a foundation for future commercial ties. India had announced that a target has been set to double the India-Malaysia trade in the next three years from the present level of $2.5 billion. Similarly India and ASEAN signed three agreements in Indonesia recently:

(a) a framework agreement towards a free trade area by 2012
(b) a joint declaration against terrorism
(c) India's accession to the ASEAN "Treaty of Amity and Cooperation" (TAC).

These three accords should greatly contribute to a more productive Indian relationship with Southeast Asia. By far the most important agreement among the three is on the framework for a free trade area by 2012. What is particularly commendable is the clear time frame, the interim steps and the realistic goals that have been agreed to by India and the ASEAN group of countries. India has also shown some economic magnanimity and not demanded reciprocity at every level. For instance, while India will remove tariffs on 105 items on a common list within three years, so will Singapore, Thailand, Indonesia, Brunei, Malaysia and Philippines. The weaker economics of Cambodia, Laos, Myanmar and Vietnam have been given a time period of six years. India has also indicated that an "open skies" accord is being reached with ASEAN countries. As a first step India has offered airlines from ASEAN countries free daily services without any prior bilateral agreement. Predictably the campaign against terrorism is the second plank of India's close relationship with the region. A joint declaration against terrorism with the ASEAN assumes special significance given that Indonesia (Bali) witnessed a major terrorist attack in October 2002. The joint declaration proposed greater cooperation in legal matters, information exchange as well as closer collaboration in enforcement of anti-terrorist measures, institutional capacity building and training to combat this scourge. The free trade agreement and the declaration on terrorism are embedded in the ASEAN Treaty of Amity and Cooperation that India has also signed recently. Significantly China which like India is a dialogue partner in the grouping had also joined the 1976 treaty under which members pledge respect for their independence, sovereignty and integrity of all countries, no interference in the internal affairs of one another and peaceful settlement of intra-regional disputes. The treaty was amended in 1998 to allow countries outside ASEAN to accede to it with the consent of all the 10 members.[4] Significantly Myanmar has also entered the ASEAN block, it has signed a MoU with India in 1994 recognizing certain border trading points between Myanmar and India. The opening of 160 km Tamu-Kalay- Kalewa road in February, 2001, the opening of the Myanmar-India Friendship Centre at Yangon and the signing of a bilateral trade agreement between India and Myanmar in October, 2003, the bilateral trade agreements between India and China and the ASEAN block respectively in October, 2003 are likely to play a major role in improving the regional economic cooperation between the three countries.

Impact on the Northeastern Region of India

The Northeast region of India comprises of eight states namely, Arunachal Pradesh, Assam, Manipur, Meghalaya, Mizoram, Nagaland, Sikkim and Tripura and. The Northeast has common borders with China, Bangladesh, Bhutan and Myanmar. The region is deprived of benefits of common markets and economic opportunities due to isolation on political considerations. Despite easy access to large markets and vibrant economies the region is land locked. The people of the region belong to the races of Indo-Tibetan, Indo-Burmese, Mongolian and Mon-Khmer origin. It is these or subtypes of these races that inhibit China and the entire

Southeast Asian region – China, Myanmar, Thailand, Malaysia, Singapore, Laos, Cambodia, Vietnam, Indonesia and even Brunei. There is an amazing phonetic similarity between Malay and many of the languages spoken by the people of Northeast. Half of the species of reptiles in the zoological park in Malaysia are native to Southeast Asia and to the different states of the Northeast. The landscape is the same-lusty green, food habits are quite similar and culturally there are several resemblances. The Northeast offers many opportunities for a social and commercial integration with the Far East and the union will definitely reap huge profits for India. The frontier tribal convention organized by eighteen ethnic tribal groups on April 9-0, 1998, at Margherita in Assam demanded that the Stilwell road be opened to maintain the traditional economic and cultural relations with their original homeland where live their kith and kin.[5] If regional cooperation can be established through the various bilateral and multi lateral agreements all participating countries will be immensely benefited. The ability of a country particularly the more isolated communities within a country to participate in trade depends on the quality of transport and communication infrastructure that allows them access to the world trading system. A modern transport network between India and ASEAN can only break existing impediments. The improvement of the transport network between India and ASEAN includes construction of railways, roads and airways. For example, the construction of a Trans Asian railway route, which will connect the Lekhapani railway head in Assam, India with Kunming in South China through Myitkyina in Myanmar can be considered as proposed by the Economic and Social Commission for Asia and Pacific (hereinafter ESCAP). The 1360 km India-Myanmar-Thailand highway, the construction work of which was to be started from early 2005 at the cost of 4700 million USD will go a long way in improving the trade relationship between India and ASEAN countries.

With regard to the development of land routes for promoting regional cooperation between these countries, the reopening of the famous Stilwell Road is of utmost importance. This is the land route connecting India with Myanmar and China which was constructed between 1942-43. It runs from Ledo in Assam, India and passes through Lekhapani-Pangsau pass in India, Myitkyina and Lashio in Myanmar to Kunming in Yunnan province of China. Since Kunming is already connected with Hong Kong by an express highway, Northeast India and for that matter India as a whole could establish a direct road link with Hong Kong if the Stilwell Road is well developed. Only a short stretch of the Stilwell Road from Ledo in India to Myitkyina (403 kms) in Myanmar needs rebuilding as the stretch from Myitkyina up to Kunming has been well developed. From Myitkyina this road takes a shorter turn towards Lashio via Bhamo and from Lashio it takes a northeastern turn towards Kunming. Since Lashio is well connected (by road and rail) with central and southern provinces of Myanmar bordering Laos and Thailand, the Stilwell road can connect Northeast India with the entire Southeast Asian region. Thus if the Stilwell Road is constructed as a Trans-Asian express way and along with it if a Trans-Asian railway line is constructed then in near future the Northeast of India and for that matter the entire region could have direct assess by both road and railway not only to Myanmar and South China but also to the entire Southeast Asian region. From the eastern borders of Arunachal Pradesh exports from India could reach Kunming in south China by the Stilwell Road covering a distance of nearly 1079 miles within two days, Yangon in Myanmar within two and half days, Bangkok in four days and Singapore in five to six days. This land route for trade would be shorter and cheaper in comparison to the existing sea routes.

South Asia has tremendous opportunities which it can utilize to its full potential. These resources include the rich and varied human resources, a population younger than the world average, growing knowledge economies and an increasing purchasing power of the collective market. Other complementary strengths of the region include the efficient exploitation of the synergies to enhance intra-regional trade, the massive untapped capacities for hydro-power and unexploited hydrocarbons, rich diversity of bio-resources and combined political weight and economic strength that could give considerable leverage in pursuing the objective of a multipolar world order. Being geographically contiguous Northeast India can produce most of the ingredients that are used in the South Asian cuisine at half the cost. The export of celery, bamboo shoot, *kaffur*, lime and other such produce can substantially lift the agriculture sector of Northeast India. Specialized outsourcing of handicrafts and other similar projects from these countries to the Northeast can truly boost the small scale and cottage industry sector. The Northeast has huge untapped reserves of uranium and coal, thick forests and plantations. Malaysian timber which travels across Northeast India to be manufactured at Delhi may well be sawn and treated in the timber treating mills scattered around the Margherita area of Assam. The plywood factories in Upper Assam can come alive once again by using Malaysian timber for manufacturing plywood. It was highly symbolic that the India-ASEAN Car Rally was flagged off from Guwahati. The rally was initiated in the wake of a Framework Agreement for Comprehensive Economic Cooperation between India and the ASEAN (hereinafter CECA) that aims to integrate India and the ASEAN into a Regional Trade and Investment Area (hereinafter RITA) in the long run, through progressive liberalization of trade in goods and services and facilitation of investment. The significance of the car rally lies in the reality that the

Northeast is indeed the gateway to Southeast Asia and it is in this part of India that efforts for greater Indo-ASEAN economic integration have to start. From here one meanders into the larger ASEAN panorama. In this background, the recent developments towards establishing Indo-ASEAN FTA, BIMSTEC FTA, India-Thailand FTA, India Singapore FTA, India-Malaysia trade agreements raise new hopes and provide new opportunities for the development of the Northeast region based on external trade.

Conclusion

India's trade has dramatically changed from west to east since countries of this region have embraced globalization. Though India's trade with ASEAN has been increasing there is enough scope to raise it further based on the existing potentialities. In this respect regional cooperation with ASEAN will play an important role. It is true that there will be some external diseconomies but one has to agree with the point that these external diseconomies will be much smaller than the immense benefit which would come from the regional cooperation through trade. To achieve such regional economic cooperation through trade the physical linkages among the trading partners in the form of trans-national roadways, railways, waterways and airways are essential. The active participation and financial cooperation among all trading countries and international financial institutions by bearing the huge amount of capital expenditure needed to build such infrastructure facilities will be highly appreciable.

REFERENCES

1. *Centre for Monitoring Indian Economy* (CMIE) Pvt. Ltd, "Foreign Trade and Balance of Payments", August, 2004, Mumbai, India.
2. *Ibid.*
3. *Ibid.*
4. *Ibid.*

5. Barua, Pratim: "Trade Opportunities for India vis-à-vis South East Asia, with special reference to China, Myanmar and Bangladesh (Recent Trends)", paper presented at the *International Conference on Regional Cooperation*, Margherita, January 18-19, 2004.
6. Borbora, Saundariya and Mahanta, Ratul: "Border Trade with Bangladesh: Opportunities for Economic Development in Assam", *Indian Journal of Economics*, 85th Conference Volume, 2002.

Sources Cited

1. Bora, S.: "Initiating a Cooperative Regime: Moving from Suspension to Trust", paper presented at the 9th UGC sponsored Refresher Course in Economics, held at Dibrugarh University, Assam, December 21, 2004 - January 9, 2005.
2. Bhaumik, T.K.: "India-ASEAN Trade Integration: the North Eastern Gateway", www.google.com.
3. Chongli, Wang: "Developing and Promoting the Trade Relationship between China and India", paper presented at the International Seminar on *Regional Development in India and China*, New Delhi, November 19-20, 1998.
4. Coopers and Lybrand: *Assam: A Guide for Investors*, Report submitted to the Government of Assam, 1996.
5. Goswami, H. and Gogoi, Jayanta Kr.: "Regional Cooperation between China, Myanmar, Bangladesh and India through bilateral trade: Impact on North East India", *Assam Economic Journal*, Vol. XVI, 2003.
6. *Research and Information System*, "India's Border Trade with Select Neighboring Countries", New Delhi, 1996.
7. Seminar papers on *Border Trade in North East India: Perspective, Issues and Problems*, organized by the North East India Council for Social Science Research, Shillong, India. December 14-15, 1998.
8. *Transforming the North East*, High Level Commission Report to the Prime Minister of India, Government of India, Planning Commission, New Delhi, March 1997.

9. Yumnam, Amar: "Indo-Myanmar Trade through Moreh: Time to Show, Time to Reap", paper presented at the seminar on *Trans-Border Trade in North East India*, Society for Conflict Analysis and Resolution, New Delhi and OKD Institute of Social Change and Development, held at Gujarat, India, July 28, 1999.

10

ENDORSING TOURISM: A RESOURCE FOR THE NORTHEAST

Charles Reuben Lyngdoh

Tourism in simple terms is the activity of undertaking a journey for recreation. The term "Tourism" is related to 'tour' which has been derived from the Latin word "*Tornos*" (turner's wheel), it also means a 'round tour'.[1] It is used in the sense of traveling from one place to another, the journey of which includes visiting a number of tourist centres in one succession covering places of the region or country. Thus a meaningful interpretation of the term should include the study of places, the tourist and the associated infrastructural features that support tourism. Tourism involves travel that is of a temporary nature. It should be voluntary and should not have remunerative employment as its aim.[2] According to the 'International Union of Official Travel Organisation', a tourist is a person traveling for a period of twenty four hours or more in the host country other than that in which he normally works and resides (U.N. Conference, 1963). Another view regards a 'tourist' as a temporary visitor who stays at least 24 hours in another country or region for recreation, health, study, pilgrimage, sports, business, meeting and family purposes.[3]

In the case of India a tourist is further classified into a 'foreign' and 'domestic' tourist. A foreign tourist is a person visiting India on a foreign passport staying for a duration of not less than twenty-four hours and not more than six months, the purpose of whose journey can be classified as under:

(a) Leisure- recreation, holiday, health, study
(b) Business, family, music, meeting.

The following categories of travelers are not included as foreign tourists:

(a) Nationals of Nepal entering India through land routes along the Indo-Nepal border
(b) All foreigners entering India from Bhutan by land
(c) Children aged less than three years.

A domestic tourist on the other hand is one who travels within India to a place other than his/her usual place of residence, at least for the distance of 80 kms one way, stays at hotels or other rented places, uses the sight seeing facilities for a duration of not less than twenty-four hours or one night and not more than six months for the purpose above stated.[4]

Thus tourism as a journey includes within its ambit an extraordinarily wide range of services. It encompasses all the activities (business or leisure) of persons traveling to and staying in places outside their usual environment for a fixed period of time. The activities of a tourist traveler demand for goods and services and the establishments which provide such services are considered a part of the tourism industry. Tourism today is acknowledged as one of the biggest industries in the world and is perhaps growing faster than any other industry. Tourism represents 40% of all exports of services, making it one of the largest categories of international trade. In 2005 international tourism receipts reached 682 billion dollars and more than 800 billion when airline tickets are included. This trade volume equals or exceeds that of oil exports, food products, or even cars. The growth of tourism as an industry is phenomenal simply for the fact that it exhibits the "multiplier effect". Thus tourism in the core itself affects more than thirty odd sectors of activity which include amongst others, hotels, food and beverage, surface transport, aviation, sports and recreation and handloom and handicraft.

Tourism is a powerful instrument of economic progress which has contributed to the turnaround and growth of several economies around the world. Its contribution to the world economy both in terms of GDP growth (10.6% in 2005) and employment generation is spectacular (221.568 million in 2005).[5] Tourism is one of the fastest growing sectors and this has been forcefully stated in the forecasts of the World Tourism Organization (WTO). According to the projections of the WTO, income from tourism excluding transport will touch a staggering USD 2 trillion by the year 2020. Tourism today is a much favored economic activity both in developed and developing nations. It carries immense hope for socio-economic improvement for the countries in the developing world. It is a faster activity of generating employment, both skilled and unskilled especially for the disadvantaged sections of society helping to achieve the vision of an inclusive economic growth. China has impressed the world by recording 46.81 million arrivals in the year 2005 standing fourth among the list of top ten countries in international tourist arrivals.[6] Two decades ago the figures of tourist arrivals in China were almost the same as those of India. China's remarkable success in promoting tourism has been achieved by according national priority to the systematic development of its tourism potential, coordinating the establishment of airports, highways, hotels, shopping malls, entertainment centers and eateries while simultaneously dovetailing with industrial and business development.[7]

ABLE 10.1

Tourist Arrivals in India from Neighbouring Countries in 2004[8]

Country	*Total*	*Male*	*%*	*Female*	*%*	*Unreported*	*%*
Bangladesh	477446	351878	73.7	116974	24.5	8594	1.8
Bhutan	7054	3979	56.4	1855	26.3	1220	17.3
Malaysia	84390	49368	58.5	29115	34.5	5907	7.0
Myanmar	4932	2959	60.0	1564	31.7	409	8.3
Singapore	60710	36062	59.4	19852	32.7	4796	7.9
Thailand	33442	15550	46.5	12541	37.5	5351	16.0

In the backdrop of the phenomenal growth of the tourism industry especially in the South Asia and Asia Pacific Region, it becomes imperative to situate the northeastern part of India in the tourist map of this region. In 2005 Asia and the Pacific region received 156.7 million tourist arrivals, rating the region second only to Europe which received 441.6 million tourist arrivals.[9] The northeastern part of India, Paradise Unexplored, a term in common parlance referring to the region of the country comprising of eight states: Arunachal Pradesh, Assam, Manipur, Meghalaya, Mizoram, Nagaland, Sikkim and Tripura is unique in various ways. Nature has endowed this part of the country with an abundance of resources. This northeastern region also displays a rich mosaic of distinct yet diverse cultures and communities some of which possess very rare, time tested unique characteristics. Moreover, this part of the country is advantageously located at the egress to South Asia and Southeast Asia.

This locational proximity could be channeled to draw maximum benefits for promoting tourism in all the northeastern states. Every single creative activity initiated whether it is promoting tea plantations, tribal habitat, herbal medicine, international trade fairs, world record shattering events and so on, could inevitably lead to tourism promotion. In addition to being extremely labor intensive the tourism industry is also a service industry capable of generating manifold employment opportunities to address this growing problem in all the states. It is therefore essential to create facilities and develop professionalism in order to tap the maximum potential of this industry. Development of infrastructure should be accorded priority, effective marketing and promotional efforts need to be undertaken to attract both the domestic and foreign tourists and training local youth in various tourism related vocations should be undertaken on a priority. Planning for sustainable development of tourism therefore involves an integrated development of basic infrastructure and amenities along with development of tourism facilities in a balanced manner.

TABLE 10.2

Classification of Foreign Tourists According to Purpose of Visit in 2004[10]

Country	*Total*	*Reason For Visit*			
		Business	*Conference*	*Education / Employment*	*Tourism / others*
Bangladesh	477446	4774 (1.0)	955 (0.2)	955 (0.2)	470762 (98.6)
Bhutan	7054	99 (1.4)	42 (0.6)	71 (1.0)	6842 (97.0)
Malaysia	84390	1604 (1.9)	253 (0.3)	506 (0.6)	82027 (97.2)
Myanmar	4932	123 (2.5)	30 (0.6)	44 (0.9)	4735 (96.0)
Singapore	60710	2611 (4.3)	182 (0.3)	182 (0.3)	57735 (95.1)
Thailand	33442	870 (2.6)	234 (0.7)	401 (1.2)	31937 (95.5)

Note: Figures in parentheses show percentage to total.

The tourism industry generates substantial economic benefits to both host countries and tourists' home countries. Especially in developing countries, one of the primary motivations for a region to promote itself as a tourism destination is the expected economic improvement. Tourism can induce the local government to make infrastructure improvements such as better water and sewage systems, roads, electricity, telephone and public transport networks, all of which can improve the quality of life for residents as well as facilitate tourism. It has been thus appropriately observed that tourism not only needs to grow but also needs to develop. Tourism is an information-intensive industry, its success greatly depends on the education and awareness of the host community. Improving access to and the quality of basic education in point of origin as well as destination areas should be a priority. Investment in professional training and capacity building at the local level is essential to ensure equitable distribution of its benefits to local populations.

TABLE 10.3

Domestic and Foreign Tourists Visits to the Northeast (2002–2004)[11]

State	*2002*			*2003*			*2004*		
	Domestic	*Total*	*Foreign*	*Domestic*	*Total*	*Foreign*	*Domestic*	*Total*	*Foreign*
Arunachal Pradesh	4372	4559	187	2195	2318	123	4740	5009	269
Assam	1953915	1960324	6409	2156675	2163285	6610	2288093	2295378	7285
Manipur	89633	89854	221	92923	93180	257	93476	93725	249
Meghalaya	268609	271755	3146	371953	378257	6304	433495	445902	12407
Mizoram	29417	29676	259	35129	35408	279	38598	38924	326
Nagaland	14263	14920	657	5605	6348	743	10056	11140	1084
Sikkim	159342	167908	8566	179661	191627	11966	230719	245365	14646
Tripura	260586	263188	2602	257331	260527	3196	260907	264078	3171
India	269598028	274755546	5157518	309038335	315746814	6708479	366221248	374518231	8296983

Rural Tourism

Rural tourism is a form of tourism that is promoted in the countryside away from urban populated centres. It includes a range of activities, services and amenities provided by farmers and rural people to attract tourists to their area in order to generate extra income for their businesses.[12] The remoteness and solitude of the countryside provide the tourist with a healthy environment and the opportunity to experience the vast trove of treasures associated with the particular place. Rural tourism includes amongst others:

(a) *heritage tourism:* a visit to experience a place or an activity that has strong links with the past
(b) *nature based ecotourism:* a visit to a natural area to enjoy the scenery, topography or to even participate in adventurous activities
(c) *agritourism:* a visit to a work farm, an agricultural, horticultural or agribusiness operation for recreation, education or involvement in related activities.

Rural tourism can be sustained. It attracts a smaller number of visitors who are interspersed across a number of rural destinations, it does not require extensive infrastructural development, it allows the tourist to come in contact with local culture and tradition while personally interacting with local residents and above all it injects the tourist's purchasing power directly into the rural economy. Rural tourism provides an incentive for infrastructural development which contributes to the growth of other economic activities in rural areas.

The Northeast has tremendous latent prospective to promote rural tourism. Rural tourism possesses an array of endowments to connect the visitors from the frenetic present and mesmerize them with the traditional assets of communities whose domain lies off the beaten track.[13] Rural tourism should be seen as an economic activity having the possibility of opening up significant opportunities for economic value addition for rural areas in the region which can be achieved with minimal investment. It can become an important means of earning additional income which can help overcome the seasonality of the incomes of the rural population. It is important to integrate rural tourism with established mainline tourist circuits to derive maximum benefits. The following villages have been highlighted in the rural tourism circuit of the Northeast:

Assam: Durgapur in Golaghat District, Sualkuchi in Kamrup District
Sikkim: Lachen in North District
Tripura: Kamalasagar in West Tripura District.[14]

Tuophema, a village approximately 41 kms from Kohima today distinctly features in the tourist circuit of Nagaland. The village community in Touphema has ingeniously developed and maintained a tourist village integrated with all the modern amenities in an ethnic ambiance.

Promoting rural tourism in the Northeast requires comprehensive planning and development to ensure that the people develop appropriate humanitarian attitudes, social values and knowledge to be able to effectively use the resources around them thereby ensuring the welfare of the present and the future.

Homestay experience should be an integral part of rural tourism. It allows the tourist to feel the pulse of traditional hospitality while visiting rural Northeast. An open minded visitor will definitely be exposed to a fascinating culture and village style living first hand. The *Kampung* or traditional village is a classic example of homestay tourism being promoted across Malaysia. It allows the visitor to establish a bond with her/his friendly foster family, to get acquainted with the village and the village elders and above all to experience the traditional Malay charm that has been preserved throughout the ages and is still very much alive.[15] The concept of homestay supports community based activities that relate to tourism. Living with these friendly kampung folks will expose visitors to many unique practices such as the ability to eat with hands, wearing a comfortable *sarong* and playing kites with children amidst the scenic paddy fields. Due to their participation the kampung folks are the primary recipients of benefits derived from these programmes. The guests of these homestay programmes can experience and participate in local community activities such as cooking classes, attending a traditional Malay wedding, watching a local cultural dance or even participating in the mesmerising *silat*, a form of local martial arts.[16] There are approximately 1200 families participating in the homestay programme involving 25 *kampungs* all around Malaysia.

Health and Medical Tourism

Health tourism is a form of activity which provides 'cost effective' private medical care in collaboration with the tourism industry for patients needing surgical and other forms of specialized treatment.[17] It is becoming a popular form of vacationing as it mixes leisure, fun and relaxation along with wellness and healthcare. A combination of many factors has lead to the recent increase in popularity of health tourism especially in developing countries. Exorbitant cost of healthcare and medical facilities in advanced countries, easy and affordability of international travel, favorable currency exchange rates in the global economy, rapidly improving technology and high standards of medical care, existence of tourist circuits and places of interest along with necessary support services have all contributed their share to this rapid development of medical tourism.

Though India has traditionally been a preferred destination for Yoga, Ayurveda and herbal medicine, it is only in recent times that it has captured the attention foreign tourists as an allopathic health destination. Today India is recognized as one of the most important hubs for health tourism. Indian healthcare is witnessing an increasingly strong participation of the corporate and the private sector which not only provides world class medical services but is also backed by a highly educated specialized set of professionals. India thus has tremendous potential to promote health tourism. India needs to leverage this competitive edge especially its cost advantage. The Confederation of Indian Industry (CII) points out that while a heart surgery in the US costs US$ 30,000 in India it costs US$6000. Similarly a bone marrow transplant in the US costs US$ 2,50,000 while in India it costs US$ 26,000.[18] The Northeast should also seriously consider itself as a health destination especially for its international neighbors. The establishment of new institutes such as the North Eastern Indira Gandhi Regional Institute of Health and Medical Sciences (NEIGRIHMS) at Shillong is a step in this direction. NEIGRIHMS is an autonomous institute established by Government of India in 1987 under the Meghalaya Registration of Societies Act 1983. It is the first and only postgraduate medical institute in the northeastern region and third in the country established by Ministry of Health and Family Welfare, Government of India and has been categorized as a "super specialty" hospital. Its objective is to impart health services to the people of the region under four pillars:

(a) Medical Education & Human Resource Development

(b) User Friendly Patient Care System with State-of-Art Technology

(c) Central Research Organization with Primary and Advanced Research Facilities

(d) Health Consultancy Service in Regional and Central Health Schemes

It is a 1000-bedded hospital presently having a number of operational departments such as cardiology, gastroenterology, pathology, pediatrics, radiology and imaging. The departments proposed to be set up include neurology, nephrology, medical oncology, urology amongst others. There are also plans to set up a 100-bedded cancer hospital in the campus along with a full fledged Ayurvedic Medical College and Nursing College.

The region is also known for its age old practice and tradition of herbal health. The potential of this alternative needs to be seriously considered especially when there are practitioners of international repute. Health and medical tourism needs to be aggressively marketed to the international neighbors in conjunction with the tourism industry as there exists a significant scope to promote cross border, patiently friendly medical services.

Conventions and Conferences

Today MICE (Meetings, Incentives, Conventions and Exhibitions) tourism has witnessed a paced development across the world with a potential of generating revenue to the tune of US$ 280 billion. This segment depends on large capacity convention centres, professional staff, a rich cuisine and a host of add on facilities. Its clients include decision-makers and the drivers of trade, business and economic activity both at the national and international level. A number of state capitals in the northeast have inadvertently become popular cities for holding conferences and conventions. The thought of Shillong as a sought after MICE destination is not a distant dream but an impending reality. Any such destination should have the reputation of hosting exciting, well-run and successful MICE events. Thailand is an attractive meeting and conference destination in the Southeast Asia region for a number of reasons –

(a) Bangkok is easily accessible and serves as a regional aviation hub

(b) accommodation boasts of a wide range of hotels and resorts at major MICE destinations of Bangkok, Phuket, Chiang Mai, Pattaya and Hua Hin

(c) activities are never ending, be it culture, exotic tours across the varied landscape, luxury spa and so on

(d) hospitality is well known and service ever friendly

(e) marvelous Thai and international cuisines to suit varied taste buds

(f) professional and experienced staff, well organized, stylish and popular events

(g) plenty of shopping in the centre of Asia for branded goods as well as for traditional handicrafts

(h) Thailand has also been a safe destination for visitors.[19]

These destinations in the Northeast need to gear themselves to this reality by quickening the pace of building new accommodation to cater to the standard and class demands of conference and convention destinations.

Lessons from Kerala

1. Tourism in Kerala has been declared an industry since 1986. Budgetary support has also increased accordingly. Large scale private investment has also been attracted to the State to assist the growth of tourism.
2. The Tourism department actively participates in national as well as international trade fairs showcasing the uniqueness of Kerala as a tourist

destination – heritage/ cultural/ religious tourism, backwater tourism, beach tourism, hill station tourism, forest and wildlife tourism, ayurvedic tourism.

3. The department has prepared a 20 year plan for tourism development in the State. Such a plan is a necessity to have a vision, a target, a strategy and an action plan to sustain tourism in the long term.
4. Kerala has been declared as one of the "Must See" destinations of a life time by National Geographic Traveller.
5. It has also been declared as one of the 100 "Great Trips" of the 21st century by Travel and Leisure.

Positive Vibrations

The states of the Northeast also need to organize mega events to attract the attention of the world. The Meghalaya Tourism Development Forum (MTDF) a non-governmental organization committed to promoting tourism in the State, organized "Positive Vibrations" at Shillong on October 28th, 2006, a drum ensemble intended to break the existing world record of a performance of 7727 drummers held by the Po Leung Kuk Charity of Hong Kong. Michael Sean Witty the adjudicator for this event in Shillong from the Guinness Book of World Records was especially flown in from England. The participants at Shillong numbering 7951 in an orchestrated and synchronized manner drummed their way into a new world record amidst the thunderous cheer and euphoria of the considerable gathering of visitors. The success of this drum ensemble is attributed to human ingenuity, perseverance and clarity of focus of all those involved in its preparation and execution – R.G. Lyngdoh, the then Minister, Tourism, Government of Meghalaya, the Directorate of Tourism, Government of Meghalaya, the MTDF the organizer of this ground-breaking event and above all the enthusiastic participation of myriad groups and individuals. Meghalaya and in particular Shillong has been permanently etched in the annals of tourist destinations with this feat. The tourism departments and organizations promoting tourism in the northeastern states should endeavor to materialize similar innovative ideas to promote tourism.

The Consecrated Festival

The month of December rekindles powerful images associated with Christmas: infant Jesus in a manger with Mary and Joseph, the three Magi and the Guiding Star, the Christmas tree, Santa Claus and Christmas presents, Christmas carols on cold winter nights ...... the list of images are endless. States in the Northeast with a sizeable Christian population could effectively tap the potential of this chilly season with the warmth and hospitality of its people. Visitors and tourists would be welcome to witness and even partake in the activities associated with this festival of birth and hope. They would indeed be warmly received in the hearths and homes of the people of the region.

Promoting tourism during the month of December has not received the desired attention of governments of the region. The idea of a Christmas journey and a Christmas holiday package to the Northeast should definitely be on the itinerary of tourism endorsement. This form of tourism requires the minimum investment but has the potential to produce the maximum appreciation from the tourist. It is tourism where the host embraces the traveler with his/her warmth and hospitality commensurate with the season of joy, peace and love. All the sentiments associated with the season find exquisite expression in the various activities. *Atithi Devo Bhava* finds true expression in Christian homes of the region during the season of yuletide.

Suggestions

To ensure that tourism becomes a resource for the region the following proposals may be considered:

(a) Promoting tourism should be matched by actual budgetary support by the respective states.

(b) Tourism policies should be evolved by respective states. Investment subsidies should be accorded in tourism related activities.

(c) Tourism departments/corporations of different states should also frequently participate in different tourist fairs and marts in both the national as well as the international level. Tourism fairs should also be organized in the respective state capitals of the Northeast on a rotational basis.

(d) Aggressive marketing of the region in other parts of the country as well as in the neighboring country capitals.

(e) Guwahati airport should be developed into a state of the art airport with night landing, refueling, and service and maintenance facilities. The open skies policy should usher in the element of competitiveness in the aviation market. Old air strips dotting different parts of the Northeast should also be revived to increase air connectivity.

(f) Travel advisories in neighboring countries should be encouraged to paint a positive image of the region.

(g) A regional passport office should also be opened in Silchar to cater to the demands of people in the southern region of the Northeast. Opening counselor offices of at least some of our eastern neighbors in Guwahati and Silchar should be considered.

(h) Visa restrictions could also be relaxed, visa on arrival in Guwahati especially for visits to the region could also be considered.

(i) We need to have a paradigm shift in our attitudes towards people visiting us.

(j) Government rest houses/inspection bungalows especially in interior areas should also be given out to tourists.

(k) A number of states in the region have implemented the Inner Line Permit, the Restricted Area Permit and the Protected Area Permit. These are some of the problems that we face and we cannot do away with them. The initiative to relax the rules and regulations of these permits has to come from the respective state governments and from the people involved in promoting tourism in the region.

(l) Respective states should also consider developing east-west corridors within their own states to increase intra-state surface connectivity.

(m) Tourist circuits should be made operational on a regular basis. Tourists should stay at least two weeks in the region to enjoy the beauty of the region. This will also ensure that no single tourist spot or area is over exploited by mass tourism.

(n) Awareness should be created about what tourism is at the school, college and even at the level of the community. We need to encourage active community participation because they are the main stake owners of community resources.

Tourism Strategy and the Seven S's

Swagat (hospitality)
Soochna (information)
Suvidha (facilitation)
Suraksha (safety)
Sahyog (cooperation)
Sanrachna (infrastructure development)
Safai (cleanliness)

Conclusion

Tourism is an external articulation of humankind's natural instinct to travel, to experience, to savor, to meet and learn...... combining the elements of adventure, education and entertainment. Endorsing tourism in the Northeast should be the incentive catalyst for peace and understanding among the people. It should simultaneously reconcile the pressing need for environment conservation with the urgent demand for economic development and upliftment from the binds of poverty. It should promote a respect for ethical values of the host communities showcased while such communities should acclimatize themselves with the needs and expectations of the visitor.

If tourism is to be sustained awareness should be created at different levels of the community about the vast and untapped possibilities of this activity. Promoting tourism in the Northeast should be "*low impact-high value*". Governments of the Northeast must play the role of initiators in identifying, investing and prioritizing key tourist destinations in their respective states. Their policies should also facilitate the creation of a healthy investment climate to attract private participation. We lack nothing in beauty or in hospitality. What we lack is in fact an insight to realize that we are the owners of the tourist resources around us. We have yet to reap the potentials of these resources. The tourism we promote in the region should endorse sustainability, conservation and involvement. Tourism should never be considered an alternative but rather, a way of life.

REFERENCES

1. Rai, Harish Chandra: *Hill Tourism: Planning and Development*, Kanishka Publishers, New Delhi, 1998.
2. *Ibid.*
3. Zulfikar, Mohammed: *Introduction to Tourism and Hotel Industry with special focus on Front Office Management*, Vikas Publishing House Pvt. Ltd., New Delhi, 1998.
4. *Ibid.*
5. *Figures 2005 Incredible India*: Ministry of Tourism, Government of India, New Delhi, August 2006.
6. *Ibid.*
7. *Safari India*: Vol XXV, No. 9, September 2002, Reeti Printers and Publishers, New Delhi, 2002.
8. *India Tourism Statistics* 2004: Market Research Division, Ministry of Tourism & Culture, Government of India, 2006.
9. *Figures 2005 Incredible India*: *op.cit.*
10. *Ibid.*
11. *India Tourism Statistics* 2004: *op.cit.*
12. *The Concept of Rural Tourism* - http://www.ratztamara.com/rural.html
13. *Rural Tourism in India*: Incredible India, www.incredibleindia.org, June 2006.
14. *Ibid.*
15. *Malaysia Truly Asia: Homestay* – Tourism Malaysia
16. http://virtualmalaysia.com/destination/homestay
17. *Need for Medical Tourism*:

    http://www.health-tourism-india.com/need-for-medical-tourism.html
18. "India a World Class Medical Tourist Destination": *Travel Span*, Vol. 5, Issue 6, August 2005, Devender Grover, New Delhi.
19. "Why do MICE delegates focus on Thailand" -*Travel Span*, Vol. 3, No. 6, April 2003, Devender Grover, New Delhi

11

LOOK EAST POLICY: PROMOTING TOURISM IN THE NORTHEAST

Mousumi Borah

The Northeast comprising of the States of Arunachal Pradesh, Assam, Manipur, Meghalaya, Mizoram, Nagaland, Sikkim and Tripura is characterized by distinct agroclimatic areas ranging from humid-tropic to temperate zones. This isolated land locked region shares less than 2% of its borders with the rest of the country while more than 98% of the same is shared with Bhutan, Bangladesh, Myanmar and the Tibetan region of China.[1] This region has the potential to serve as the entrepot for the entire Indian hinterland. Yet, the reality is very disappointing. Economic development of the Northeast region has followed a specific pattern. Economic prosperity came to be concentrated in select pockets. Vast areas therefore remain inaccessible and backward and along with the perpetuation of traditional practices, select and focused development impeded the efficacy of the process of modernization in the region.[2] The reorganization and the creation of the northeastern states in a way hampered the integrated development of the region. The small, economically non-viable states and union territories are for obvious reasons unable to take up individual development projects and the Northeast does not enjoy the necessary power and resources to do so.[3]

In recent decades India has opened her economy to international trade and has launched initiatives to forge closer trade and economic ties with immediate neighbors. The cooperation between India and east Asian countries in the 21st century will definitely help to make this century the "century of Asia". With this vision, the Government of India in the 1990s promoted the Look East Policy which is now an important part of India's foreign policy. Look East Policy has a strong economic rationale. Today east Asia comprising of Japan, China, South Korea and ASEAN are India's largest trading partners ahead of the European Union and the United States. The policy launched in 1992 had its genesis in the end of the cold war following the collapse of the Soviet Union. The economic opportunities for the states of the Northeast in the context of this policy need to be looked into. India has commenced a broad economic and strategic partnership with the dynamic countries of Southeast Asia. To carry out the Look East Policy India had initiated a limited sectoral partnership with these countries in 1992 which subsequently transformed into a full dialogue partnership in 1995. It was admitted as a member of the Asian Regional Forum in 1996 and has been participating in the Indo-Asian summits since 2002. India is also involved in regional initiatives such as BIMST-EC and the Ganga Mekong Cooperation, it became a member of the East Asia Summit (EAS) in December, 2005.

In so far as the Northeast is concerned the relevance of the Look East Policy centers around the opening of continental connection through points along the 1643 km international border with Myanmar covering the four states of Arunachal Pradesh, Nagaland, Manipur and Mizoram. The land locked Northeast is ideally placed to link India with ASEAN both in the geographical and the commercial sense.

There are strong cultural and historical linkages with the East, which could be exploited and thereby lead to economic cooperation. Placing the economy of the Northeast on the path of development requires a considerable thrust. The Look East Policy provides an opportunity to solve the problem of distance from markets. It has a wide scope for promoting tourism in the region. Tourism is an industry which creates a product that does not have to depend on raw materials imported from outside. Tourism can be developed and promoted anywhere and its encouragement is an appropriate step for regional development. To ensure that the Look East Policy brings abundant economic opportunities to the region, an assessment must be made of its comparative advantages and a plan of action formulated based on these assessments. Intensive efforts to promote business synergies between India and the ASEAN countries in areas of infrastructure and tourism got a boost with the India-ASEAN Business Summit.

Historically, the Northeast had extensive links with the neighboring regions of Tibet, Bhutan, Burma and China forming the southern trail of the Silk Road. However as India became an important colony of Great Britain, barriers were erected between Bhutan and Assam, while traditional links with other countries acquired a strategic hue. Prior to 1947, the region comprising the Northeast had substantial economic and social intercourse with the neighboring countries. East Bengal (later called East Pakistan and ultimately Bangladesh) was well integrated with the Northeast. There is evidence that trade and migration into territories today comprising of the Tibet autonomous region of China, Myanmar, Yunnan province of China, Nepal, Bhutan and Sikkim, were important to the economy of the region. Since India has traditionally enjoyed many economic and strategic links with this region a trade pact with ASEAN is a very desirable step. India's Look East Policy today aims to develop her states in the Northeast by linking them to

Southeast Asia through road, rail, river and air links via Myanmar. This is part of the larger project to build Eurasian land and rail corridors that could connect Singapore to Istanbul and Europe via India and China. It needs to be emphasized that the physical infrastructure for facilitating tourism and economic links between the Northeast and the neighboring countries is largely absent. Indeed, one can argue that the links are weaker today than they were in 1947. Hence it is time to create proper infrastructure between Northeast India and its neighboring countries. On the 6th of July, 2006, the Nathu La pass in the Indo-China border connecting the Indian State of Sikkim with Yadong county on the southern border of Tibet had been formally opened for trade. It is a historical and a significant milestone in Indo-China bilateral relations after 44 long years.[4]

Tourism and the Northeast

In view of the centre's Look East Policy, an integrated Northeast tourism policy involving all the stakeholders is very desirable. Development of heritage tourism circuits, promotion of traditional handicrafts and textiles, integrated management plans and infrastructure development would lead to a positive impact in many spheres of the Northeast states. The structure of the economy in the region resembles the economy of the least developed parts of the globe with the primary sector accounting for 55-60% of the income. The secondary sector constitutes only a meager 11-16% of the total income making it India's industrially most backward region.[5] There is a vast scope for promoting tourism in the region. The region is bestowed with diverse tourist attractions and each state has its own distinctive features. The number of tourist arrivals in the state of Sikkim has increased from 21,854 in 1981 to 2,46,197 in 2004. By 2012 there is a plan to attract 10 lakh tourist per annum. A proposal is in the offing to integrate tourism and trade through the Nathu La trade route. However care should be taken to minimize the adverse impact on our society, culture, environment and economy. Sikkim is the gateway to India's Look East Policy. This policy has been influenced by the concept of regionalism triggered by globalization and flourishing people to people contact. The Government has a crucial role to play in India's trade, tourism and other areas of economic cooperation with countries in the eastern fringes including Thailand, Malaysia, Singapore, China and Japan. In the context of the Look East Policy Sikkim has three major items to offer, floriculture, horticulture and tourism. The Asian Development Bank (hereinafter ADB) has explored the growth possibilities of the Northeast region (including tourism promotion) with its South Asia Sub Regional Economic Cooperation (SASEC) initiative. It has identified the Buddhist circuit and sustainable eco-tourism as the main tourism strengths of the region. Besides emphasizing the traditional circuit of places where Lord Buddha lived, meditated, attained enlightenment and nirvana, it has integrated the Buddhist circuit concept with the SASEC concept. These attractions are likely to open up interest in the Northeast as a majority of the tourists from the Asia Pacific region are Buddhists. Similarly foreign tourists today are looking at eco tourism as an alternative to mass tourism and this concept can be easily initiated in the region. Tourism promotion in the area can be enhanced with the implementation of the Look East Policy. In Sikkim, for instance, only 13% land is available for productive cultivation and the rest comprises of the Himalayas, glaciers, water bodies, flora and fauna which makes the place an ideal place for promoting eco-tourism with its broader facets like adventure tourism, village tourism and pilgrimage tourism. Nature has endowed the Northeast with enormous beauty. The tourist attractions are located and scattered all over the region especially in remote areas within highly fragile environments. In the Northeast stress should be on the creation of infrastructure in the rural areas which have a very high potential for tourism. Rural life, art, culture and heritage in rural locations and in villages which have core competency in terms of craft, handloom and textiles should be brought to the lime light.

In the present day context tourism does not confine itself to hotels, restaurants and sea beaches. It covers rural areas, the health sector and the environment. The Northeast which is endowed with scenic beauty, rich cultural heritage and unique art and craft should take full advantage of this endowment. There are about 305 communities and over 200 tribes in the region. Each community has its distinct customs, cultural heritage and folklore and as such the region has ample prospects to promote modern day tourism. The region also has several aromatic plants which could be used to develop and promote health tourism in selective locations of the region. The tourism industry can have a multiplier effect in the region. It will provide opportunities for employment, rural development and also encourage mutual co-existence through cultural exchange and thereby help in transforming a closed society to an open one. Tourism helps in the development of many subsidiary industries and services and has a huge potential to create a good many employment avenues. Tourism promotes friendship and cultural exchanges among the different countries. Though the Northeast is culturally very rich yet it remains unknown to the outside world, including the rest of India. India's Look East Policy can thus help the region to promote tourism. Cultural tourism and marketing of crafts and textiles can serve as a powerful catalyst for preserving the ongoing viability of both the tangible and the intangible heritage of the Northeast. As the region is geographically isolated from the rest of India, accessibility of markets is a problem. However the very nature of the tourism industry brings markets to the region thereby solving the problem of availability and accessibility. The prospects and potential of promoting tourism in the Northeast have not been fully exploited. A significant portion of the region is still unexplored. The modern day tourist seeks unique experiences and this region can earn in millions from this industry. In addition to promoting international tourism the region should also exploit the prospects of regional and domestic tourism. As the Northeast is situated far away from the main entry point of tourists it is at a disadvantageous position and hence cannot attract many foreign tourists. The Look East Policy can change this entire scenario. It has been forecasted that by 2020 the Asia Pacific region will be the 2nd largest tourist generating market in the world. The projection shows that by 2020 the region will generate 405 million tourists of the total of 1561 million tourists. The Northeast should focus on the cultural, historical and ethnic links it has with these countries and thereby encourage the flow of people from these regions. By using Myanmar as a bridge to economically leverage with China and the other ASEAN nations, India wants to develop her Northeast. By taking advantage of Myanmar's links with other ASEAN countries, India hopes to transform the region from a security burden to a land of economic opportunity. A high level study group set up by the Government of Sikkim, the Nathu La Study Group submitted a very comprehensive report. This report discusses the prospects of trade and tourism through the Nathu La route for the next 20 years. The income and employment effects on road side hotels and restaurants, handicrafts, transport and communication network and many other backward and forward linkages are likely to be immense. Although the Northeast has a high prospect for tourism much has not been done in this respect. Statistics show that the advantages of tourism have not been properly harnessed. This has been clearly depicted by the following statistical data which shows the insignificant arrival figures of tourists both domestic and international in the region. Tourism has not been given its due importance in the Northeast despite having a comparative advantage in this area. Most of the tourism planning in the region appears to be adhoc. The state governments have not given their full commitment to the issue. For its success, tourism requires the involvement of many agencies. For the development of the tourist product there has to be coordination and cooperation between the various government departments such as Agriculture and Horticulture, Art and Culture, Khadi and Village Industries, Forest, PWD, PHE, Tourism, Transport and so on.

TABLE 11.1

Domestic and Foreign Tourist Arrivals in India for 1999-2001[6]

	1999 *Domestic / Foreign*	*2000* *Domestic / Foreign*	*2001* *Domestic / Foreign*
Arunachal Pradesh	1008/48	9932/2044	6349/323
Assam	14336/604	891433/5954	1010651/6171
Manipur	97523/277	105167/429	76527/183
Meghalaya	159730/1971	169929/2327	178697/2390
Mizoram	27139/216	28221/235	28771/152
Nagaland	21041/119	13272/451	9946/920
Sikkim	138785/8554	143105/10409	203306/31028
Tripura	246507/335	231902/0	254912/0
All India	190671014/5832105	22106941/5893542	234200935/5427366

Source: Ministry of Tourism, 2001.

Problems and Prospects of Tourism in the Northeast

Development of tourism leads to generation of income and employment. Tourism in the Northeast suffers from vital drawbacks like poor internal communication between the states and lack of an organizational set up. There is a lack of connectivity, lack of internal infrastructure including lodging and eating facilities, lack of a suitable standard, negative image, safety concerns with regard to insurgency and unrest. The lack of infrastructure has been responsible for the sluggish growth of industries in the region despite abundance of natural resources and endless planning to modernize the economy. Development and modernization of the Northeast has been the victim of a vicious circle.[7]

Infrastructure is crucial for the region's development to secure the benefits of promoting tourism and a free trade regime in the emerging world order. Private investment will not come up unless appropriate infrastructure is developed. Since the government's investment in infrastructure has been limited due to financial constraints foreign direct investments are required to encourage economic cooperation with Southeast Asian countries. It is important that the Indian leadership at New Delhi initiates measures for investment in infrastructure from BIMST-EC whose major thrust is development of infrastructure in the member countries. Investment in infrastructural development from BIMST-EC, promotion of tourism, development of cottage, handloom and handicraft and cane and bamboo sectors can be an important step. This will generate livelihood integration of the Northeast India with Southeast Asia.

Tourism is a major social phenomenon of modern society having far reaching economic consequences. It is an important instrument for enhancing economic development and employment generation. This fact has been well realized all over the world. There has been a substantial growth of the industry world wide and this growth is expected to swell to 1.5 billion tourists and receipts from the industry are expected to surplus US$ 200 billion. Various constraints facing the Northeast such as insurgency and absence of proper infrastructure have resulted in a poor share in revenue earnings despite huge potential. In comparison to India's share of world tourist arrivals of 0.44%, arrivals in the Northeast account for a meager 1.2% with a higher concentration in Darjeeling and Sikkim. The World Travel and Tourism Council rates India as the fastest growing tourism economy in the world. India is ranked 5th among the various hot spots. In view of the immense tourist potential the governments of the Northeast states should initiate necessary steps to tap the development of tourism in the region. The rich natural beauty, serenity, exotic flora and fauna of the region are invaluable resources for the development of eco-tourism. Road communication in the region is arduous and time consuming. Although air communication has improved it still falls short of meeting the requirements of the region. Tourism in the Northeast can be successful only when the communication to the region becomes sufficient, efficient and reliable. The Asian Highway proposes to cover a distance of 90,000 kms in twenty five countries, of which 40,000 kms will be international routes and 50,000 kms will be regional routes. If this proposal is properly planned and executed the benefits derived from this crucial communication link can change the tourism facet of the region. The Ministry of Tourism, Government of India and bodies such as the Tourism Finance Corporation of India have shown marginal interest in developing tourism within the Northeast. However 10% of the plan allocation of the Ministry of Tourism has been earmarked for the Northeast region. The financial assistance also includes assistance for promoting fairs and festivals of the northeastern states on an annual continuing basis. There is an urgent need to develop a joint North East Tourism Policy which encompasses integrated management plans, infrastructure development, marketing, publicity and promotional material, development of heritage tourist circuits and promotion of traditional handicrafts and textiles. It is suggested that the role of the government and private investors outside the region be limited to investment in infrastructural facilities and partnership in marketing. Steps have to be taken towards the development of proper connectivity within the region in terms of development of air, rail and road. The Northeast has to be incorporated in national tourism development and marketing plans. The preservation and sustainability of the tangible and the intangible heritage of the region should not be lost sight of. Unique buildings and sites need to be preserved and destruction of heritage resources needs to be stopped. To boost tourism in the region the Ministry of Tourism, Government of India has taken up some measures. For the development of human resources in tourism and hospitality education full fledged institutes of hotel management, catering technology and applied nutrition have been set up in Shillong and Guwahati respectively. In addition to offering 3 three year degree programmes in hotel management these institutes also conduct diploma courses in food and beverages services and food production. In order to give wide publicity to tourist attractions of the Northeast, the Ministry has launched nation wide campaigns on a continuing basis. This is in addition to the publicity literature which is being produced on the Northeast by the Ministry of Tourism. States of the Northeast are also given free booths in world tourism fairs.

Conclusion

Adopting a proper and integrated tourism policy requires a coordinated regional policy for entry restrictions, regulations and fees. Emphasis should be laid on long term economic gains. A policy for integrated development of adequate internal infrastructure, communication, transportation facilities should also be put in place. To remove stagnancy new technology needs to be integrated with tourism policy and planning. The entire Northeast is rich in traditional knowledge which includes not only crafts and textiles but also medicinal use of herbs and other substances, folklore and natural sciences. These knowledge based practices need to be documented and preserved. As tourism grows the Northeast has to gear up human resource development and create institutional arrangements for people's participation through public private partnership. For Northeast India the immediate necessity is to develop its transport connectivity within the region along with the urban centres through improvement of basic amenities. Unless the minimum critical requirements are present economic growth through sectors (such as tourism) which can generate effective employment opportunities will remain theoretical arguments without any tangible gains for the region. At the regional level governments need to be more active and constructive in creating a conducive climate for investment whether from within the country or from any regional forum such as BIMSTEC or the Asian Development Bank or any other transnational organizational and business entity. The region should grab the opportunity of India's Look East Policy and its geographical proximity to the dynamic Southeast Asian nations and take initiatives to promote its tourism industry. It needs to be emphasized that the physical infrastructure for facilitating tourism and economic links between the Northeast and the neighboring countries is largely absent. Indeed one can argue that the links are weaker today than they were in 1947. The Stilwell Road is now a mere muddy track and the rail links with Bangladesh stand severed. It is time to create proper infrastructure between Northeast India and its neighboring countries.

REFERENCES

1. Borah, Mousumi: "Look East Policy: Towards a new dawn", *Assam Tribune*, May 28, 2002.
2. Gopalkrishnan, R: *Socio-Political Framework in North-East India*, Vikas Publishing House Pvt. Ltd., New Delhi, 1996.
3. Bhuyan, B.C.: *Political Development of North East*, Omsons Publication, New Delhi, 1989.
4. Joshi, Dharmaraj: "The Old Silk Route", *Assam Tribune*, July 30, 2006.
5. India: *Economic Survey*, Delhi 2004.

5. India: *Economic Survey*, Delhi 2004.
6. Bezbaruah, M.P.: "Prospects for Tourism"
   http://www.india-seminar.com/2005/550/550%20m.p.%20bezbaruah.htm
7. Verghese, B.G.: *India's North East Resurgent: Ethnicity, Insurgency, Governance and Development*, Konark Publishers Pvt. Ltd., New Delhi, 1996.

12

SUSTAINING TOURISM THROUGH THE LOOK EAST POLICY

Sangita Kakoty

Introduction

Initiated in the early 1990's India's Look East Policy has begun illustrating results. India is now one of the four summit level partners (including China, Korea and Japan) of ASEAN. Trade between India and ASEAN has significantly expanded. India has signed separate Free Trade Agreements (hereinafter FTA) with Thailand and Singapore. There are plans to create a FTA with Brunei, Indonesia and Malaysia by 2011, and the remaining ASEAN countries - Philippines, Cambodia, Laos, Myanmar and Vietnam by 2016. Prime Minister Manmohan Singh's proposal for an "Asian Economic Community" to include ASEAN generated significant excitement at the 3rd ASEAN-India Summit in 2004. With India's participation in the East Asia Summit and from the level of interaction evidenced at the 4th India-ASEAN Summit, both held in Kuala Lumpur from 12-14 December, 2005 it is seen that the Look East Policy is being pursued aggressively and has started yielding results on the economic, political and strategic fields.[1] The policy which was primarily directed towards improving relations with ASEAN will now be enlarged to cover other countries of the region. In the aftermath of India's economic liberalization the Look East Policy was more than just a foreign policy alternative, as it provided a development alternative as well in synchronization with the realities of globalization and the resurgence of Asia as an economic powerhouse. To quote the Prime Minister Manmohan Singh, "*It was also a shift in India's vision of the world and India's place in the evolving global economy*". Speaking at the opening session of the 39th annual meeting of the Board of Governors of the Asian Development Bank in May 2006, the Prime Minister of India had suggested the establishment of a Pan-Asian free trade area. He also noted that his government was linking India into a web of partnerships with Asian countries through free trade and comprehensive economic cooperation agreements. As a natural corollary to its Look East initiative, India has reiterated its commitment to work with ASEAN and East Asian countries individually.

The Northeast of India

The geographical location of the northeastern region of India is of great significance in context of the Look East Policy's development on continental lines. The region shares 98% of its borders with the neighboring countries, and so, the Look East Policy can be best utilized if it seeks "*to look East, through the Northeast*". In the arena of regional cooperation the Northeast can play a pivotal role if it is geared to do so. There has been much talk about the potential of the Look East Policy transforming India's Northeast region bordering ASEAN. In this foreign policy vision the Northeast is often described as the gateway to Southeast Asia. The Look East Policy "*envisages the North-East not as a periphery of India, but as a center of thriving and integrated economic space linking two dynamic regions with a network of highways, railways, pipelines and transmission lines criss-crossing the region*". It is hoped that "*one day it will be possible to drive from Kolkata via Dhaka, or from Guwahati to Yangon and*

Bangkok in 3-4 days and that trains and buses would carry millions of tourists, pilgrims, workers and businessmen in both directions".[2] On the other hand it has been affirmatively pointed out that "*if we talk in regional terms, it cannot be through the eyes of Delhi it has to be through the eyes of the region. The Asian highway is structured to move through Imphal and Moreh in Manipur. Myanmar and Thailand have agreed to collaborate on the 700 km road that would go through the heart of Myanmar into Northern Thailand. But I do not see Upper Assam and the Stilwell road on that plan. And that is why the Kunming Initiative needs to go beyond discussions among academics and well-meaning industrialists to the field. It cannot happen on the ground if the people are not prepared and do not plan adequately. The North East is saying-This is our view, this is our stake - We cannot be just a dumping ground for Chinese goods or a corridor for Indian products. Unless we plan and strategize locally, we will not be able to connect regionally*".[3] The North Eastern Council (hereinafter NEC) has come up with several important suggestions for the development of the region. It was agreed upon that a perspective plan for the next fifteen years (up to 2020) should be visualized. This regional plan should integrate the state plan of all the states of the Northeast including Sikkim and merge these with the national objectives. The Vision NER 2020 would take into account the Government of India's "Look East Policy" initiatives in terms of communication, trade, commerce and marketing with a view to integrate the region's economy with that of Southeast Asia. There should be a paradigm shift in the planning process to involve the people at the grassroot level.

Tourism Promotion

States of the Northeast should endeavor to promote tourism. It is a fact that the Northeast of India has immense potential in the tourism sector and if developed in the proper direction with appropriate planning this industry can change the very face of the Northeast. The Draft Tourism Policy (1997) which later on took the shape of the National Tourism Policy (2002) states that—"*in context of the economic liberalization and globalization being pursued by the country, the development policies of no sector can remain static. The emergence of tourism as an important instrument for sustainable human development including poverty alleviation, employment generation, environmental regeneration and advancement of women and other disadvantaged groups in the country requires support to realize these goals*". The policy further states that- "*international tourists visiting the interiors of the country for reasons of purity of environment and nature contribute to the development of these areas, particularly the backward regions*". Thus tourism should also become a reason for better preservation and protection of our natural resources, environment and ecology.[4] The travel and tourism industry is a $32 billion industry in India today,

TABLE 12.1

Foreign Tourist Arrivals in India During 2006 (Jan-July) and Corresponding Figures for 2004 & 2005[5]

Month	*Foreign Tourist Arrivals (Nos.)*			*Percentage Change*	
	2004	*2005*	*2006**	*2005/04*	*2006/05*
January	337345	386260	444753	14.5	15.1
February	331697	389081	428325	17.3	10.1
March	293185	367068	407446	25.2	11.0
April	223884	260825	325249	16.5	24.7
May	185502	229172	262860	23.5	14.7
June	223122	258822	286257	16.0	10.6
July	272456	292345	331227	7.3	13.3
Total	1867191	2183573	2486117	16.9	13.9

* Provisional.

and accounts for 5.3% of the GDP. This industry has the potential of investment opportunities of about $8-10 billion in the next five years. A look at the statistics below would give a fair idea of the scenario–

TABLE 12.2

Foreign Exchange Earnings During 2006 (Jan-July) and Corresponding Figures for 2004 & 2005 (in Rs. Crores)[6]

Month	*Foreign Exchange Earnings*			*Percentage Change*	
	2004	*2005*	*2006**	*2005/04*	*2006/05*
January	2084.59	2326.20	2722.07	11.6	17.0
February	2049.70	2343.18	2635.98	14.3	12.5
March	1811.71	2210.62	2434.32	22.0	10.1
April	1368.42	1649.96	2127.44	20.6	28.9
May	1133.82	1452.72	1673.91	28.1	15.2
June	1363.76	1637.29	1847.26	20.1	12.8
July	776.60	2048.78	2308.98	15.3	12.7
Total	11588.60	13668.75	15749.96	17.9	15.2

* Provisional.

Foreign tourists arrivals are expected to grow to 5 million by 2007, and this figure could double to 10 million by 2012. Likewise, domestic tourists are expected to increase by 15%-20% per annum over the next five years.

Tourism in the Northeast

The eight states of the Northeast - Arunachal Pradesh, Assam, Manipur, Meghalaya, Mizoram, Nagaland, Tripura and Sikkim form part of the eastern Himalayan region which extends from Sikkim eastwards and embraces the Darjeeling hills of West Bengal. The rich natural beauty, serenity and exotic flora and fauna of the area are bounties of nature given on a platter. These can be the prime source of attraction. The rich and varied cultural mosaic showcasing the varied ethnic population is a marveled attraction. The facilities for lodging, food, shopping and entertainment are improving tremendously. The Government of India has attached great importance to the development of tourist infrastructure in the Northeast in view of the immense tourist potential that the region boasts of. Accordingly there has been a thrust on upgrading the various tourist facilities. The following steps are being taken by the Ministry of Tourism, Government of India:

(a) States of the Northeast are given free booths in the world's largest tourism fair, the International Tourist Mart, Berlin.

(b) Financial assistance for promotion of fairs and festivals is also being provided to the states of the Northeast.

(c) These states are given special focus in marketing conferences of the overseas offices of the Ministry of Tourism. These overseas offices are giving due publicity to the Northeast states for promoting tourism in the region.

Look East Policy and Tourism Initiatives for the Northeast

The vital question for the region is how to tap and convert its vast natural and human resources to promote the tourism industry? One advantage that the Northeast has is the strong historical, racial and cultural ties that it shares with Southeast Asia and also with China. The substantial prospects that the Northeast has needs to be enhanced and put into appropriate use to promote eco-tourism, cultural tourism, wildlife tourism and rural tourism. The region may not be able to immediately compete with the well developed and well equipped tourist destinations such as Bangkok and Singapore at least for the immediate future. Nevertheless it could harness and develop those sectors that it has the potential for.

States of the Northeast should strive to promote cultural tourism. To do so necessitates the construction of cultural centers and museums to showcase and celebrate the cultures of this region's diverse ethnic communities. An example of this is the Don Bosco Centre for Indigenous Cultures located at Shillong which is a must visit for any tourist visiting Meghalaya. Promoting cultural tourism will not only attract tourists but will also bring about a response to document the urge for recognition that animates the regions many ethnic movements. This will entail the formation of myriad cultural troupes performing exclusively to the interest and appreciation of the tourist clientele. The indigenous cuisine of each tribe can add to enrich the experience of the tourist traveler. Similarly accommodation facilities can also complement the cultural ambience where tourists can experience a few days in a particular culture. Rural Tourism can be incorporated as a part of cultural tourism. Tourism's growth potential can be harnessed as a strategy for rural development. The development of a strong platform around the concept of rural tourism is definitely useful for a region like the Northeast where 80% of the population resides in the villages. The stress of urban lifestyle has led to a "counter-urbanization syndrome". This has led to growing interest in rural areas. Rural tourism is one of the few activities which can provide solutions to many problems. There are other factors that are responsible for a shifting trend towards rural tourism: increasing level of awareness among people, growing interest in culture and heritage, improved accessibility and environmental consciousness. This in turn has encouraged a new trend of visiting villages to experience and live a relaxed and healthy lifestyle. The thrust should be to promote village tourism as a primary tourism product and to spread tourism and its socio-economic benefits to the rural environment. With the rich biodiversity that the Northeast is in possession of, eco tourism can be also be endorsed to its maximum potential.

Ecotourism is "*ecologically sustainable tourism with a primary focus on experiencing natural areas that foster environmental and cultural understanding, appreciation and conservation*".[7] Martha Honey defines eco tourism as "*travel to fragile pristine and usually protected areas, to strive to be low impact and (usually) small scale. It helps educate the traveler, provides fund for conservation, directly benefits the economic development and political empowerment of the local communities and fosters respect for different cultures and for human rights*".[8] Another area of interest that has tremendous potential in the Northeast is wildlife and adventure tourism. The region has a number of national parks, wildlife and bird sanctuaries that can be major tourist attractions - Kaziranga and Manas in Assam, Namdapha in Arunachal Pradesh, Keibul Lamjao in Manipur, Sephahijala in Tripura in addition to the virgin natural spots in Meghalaya and Sikkim that beckon one with the spirit of adventure. It has been suggested by the eminent journalist Sanjoy Hazarika that -"*for the time being, the Stilwell Road be marketed not as an economic route, but as an adventure package tour for tourists, to explore the natural mysticism of Dihing-Patkai, the Pangsu Pass and follow the footsteps of a legendary general.*"[9] The Ministry of Tourism in both the centre and the State of Assam is trying to promote this route though much remains to be accomplished.

With such a huge reservoir for tourism the Northeast can definitely be shaped into a tourists' haven especially for Southeast Asia. The key to this is the accessibility factor to the Northeast.

Access by Air: The Northeast is accessible by air (large aircrafts) through ten airports, of which only the Guwahati airport is an international airport (the Lokpriya Gopinath Bordoloi International Airport).

Access by rail: There are abundant train connections from all parts of the country to various destinations in the Northeast. Some of the important rail-heads are—Guwahati, New Bongaigaon, Jorhat, Tezpur, Dibrugarh town, Tinsukia, Lumding, Silchar, Dimapur and Kumarghat. Train travel is one of the most convenient and economical way to travel especially in the plain belt of Assam.

State	*Airport*
Assam	Dibrugarh
	Guwahati
	Jorhat
	Silchar
	Tezpur
Manipur	Imphal
Mizoram	Aizawl
Nagaland	Dimapur
Tripura	Agartala
West Bengal	Bagdogra

Access by Road: The states of the Northeast are served by the following National Highways: NH -31, 31B, 31C, 36, 37, 37A, 38, 39, 40, 40E, 44, 51, 52A, 52E, 53, 54 and 61. In addition there are also a number of state roads in each state. Bus services, tourist taxis and hired cars are available for road travel. All these access routes are from the west to the Northeast. In order to attract visitors and tourists from Southeast Asia road accessibility from the international borders of eastern states of India also has to improve. Why would a tourist from Myanmar, who is desirous of visiting the Northeast fly to Delhi or Kolkata and return to Guwahati the gateway to the region and then proceed on his/her onward journey to the desired destination? It would be much more attractive and convenient for such a tourist in terms of time, expenses and effort if he/she could simply cross over the international border via rail / road or fly directly into the destination of his/her choice in the Northeast. The Moreh-Tamu- Mandalay-Yangon road that brings in hundreds of vehicles and tonnes of Chinese and Southeast Asian made products to the gates of India can play a vital role in promoting tourism in the Northeast. To develop these arteries of convenient travel regional cooperation among the concerned state governments is of utmost importance. A well planned network of road, rail and air connectivity with the "east" is thus a top priority in the agenda for tourism promotion in the Northeast.

The whole concept of tourism promotion would entail the building up of sound infrastructure and communication network. Good roads, rail and air connectivity apart, upgrading the hospitality industry will be a prime necessity. Quality hotels, from three star to five star plus, bed and breakfast facilities will have to be provided to suit every kind of budget. Even the existing lodges and guest houses especially in the wildlife parks and sanctuaries will have to be upgraded if we are to cater to international tourists. A consortium of experienced travel agents and well trained tour operators will help boost the tourism scenario in the region. The overseas offices of the Ministry of Tourism can play a vital role in advertising and promoting the tourism potential of the Northeast especially in the East and Southeast Asian region. Presently there is only one such office in Singapore. Opening more information centers in the different countries will definitely help interested visitors to think and plan a trip to the Northeast. Regular tourism fairs and cultural exhibitions showcasing the Northeast in the countries of the East and Southeast Asian region will also help attract the attention of interested people. As observed by Sanjib Baruah, "*participation of the people of the region in this process is crucial. It is striking that the provincial government of China's Yunnan province and the Yunnan Academy of Social Sciences play a far more active role in China's efforts to build bridges with South and South-East Asia than their counterparts in north-east India. This is a bit ironical, since China's political system is centralized and authoritarian while ours is democratic and federal. Yet, without such participation it will be very hard to deal with certain policy challenges such as the tension between the openness of a gateway and the restrictions on land ownership and labour movement that prevail in parts of north east India"*.[10] The eminent scholar further says, "*The security prism through which official India views the North-East remains a major hurdle. It is naïve to think that ethnic festivals held under the watchful eyes of gun toting soldiers, as was the case with the Hornbill Festival in Nagaland, can ever become big tourist draws. The number of tourists who actually visit the region after working around the obstacles like the rules under the Restrictive Area Permit and Inner Line Permit remains pitifully small"*.[11] He further adds, "*counter –insurgency operations, visible army presence that is definitely not tourism friendly, and security driven restrictions will continue as long as insurgency remains and India's relations with some of our neighbours remains adversarial*".[12] Yet, India is not the only country having to reconcile security concerns with the demands of a global economy. Ensuring the security of border-crossings needs better border management, better governance inside the country as well as in the neighboring countries, deepening neighborly relations and developing multi-lateral institutions of governance. Similar views were expressed by Jairam Ramesh when he observed, "*political integrity with the rest of India, and economic integrity with the rest of Asia, with East and South East Asia particularly is certainly one direction that the North-East region must look to, as a new way of development. Clearly, the erstwhile model of economic integrity with the rest of India has not worked and is beset with a large number of logistical problems that can be solved in a short term horizon of the next 5-10 years in order to unleash the developmental potential of the aspirations of the people. But for this, mindsets in India will have to change as well, not just mindsets in North-East because we have traditionally been very suspicious of sub-regional cooperation".*[13]

The Dangers Ahead

Along with the benefits and positive aspects of tourism promotion in the Northeast, we must be aware of the probable dangers and negative aspects that might be faced as a result of promoting tourism. Tourism is one of the activities that has caused concern because of the effects of increasing human traffic on fragile environments. Countries which are looking towards tourism as a means of economic growth such as India, have limited resources and cultural restraints and they have the greatest need to pay heed to the possible negative impacts of tourism. The environmental impact of tourism is a basic issue, whether we are looking at a developed or underdeveloped area, region or country.[14] The cost of tourism for the Northeast will include extensive investment in fixed assets for infrastructure, transportation, accommodation, cultural institutions, exhibition centers and park facilities. In addition to infrastructural investment the socio-cultural costs such as additional demands on land, water, health services, creation of new jobs for displaced people, cost of positive community relationships, the disparity between the lifestyle of the visitors and those who serve them, the possible friction between local residents and the new users of valued local resources, the perception of local residents of the spending of scarce capital resource on what they consider a low priority area like tourism, will also be visible. The cultural cost of alterations in local ceremonial or traditional values, loss of privacy for local communities as tourists come to gape at their living conditions and rituals will also be immeasurable.

Tourism also causes increasing congestion and pollution as thousands of visitors flock to parks and sanctuaries in motorized vehicles. There are changes in accessibility, landscape and economic balance between man and nature. There is the cost of creating conservation zones with unforeseen or undesirable side effects, which have been observed in the eco tourism movement. The benefit of revenue from tourism does not always redress these problems but goes towards the cost of administering the project.

The tourism industry is generally self-centered and not given to educational, cultural or exchange programmes on a philanthropic basis. The natural environment even with the best will and intention in the world cannot escape damage with the increasing volume of visitors. As more and more tourists seek the exotic and the remote, the likelihood of the environment suffering becomes greater. Forests can suffer from trampling, fires, tree felling for structural facilities and waste. Wildlife suffers from loss of habitat, hunting, poaching, viewing and photography that leads to interruption of feeding and breeding patterns. Trade in wildlife trophies or tourist souvenirs is the most deliberately destructive aspect of such tourism. Again construction of tourist lodges from materials that are not integrated with the environment and the pressure they put on the land and water bodies is also willfully destructive.

Apart from these dangers related to the environment and ecology, other more social and health related problems cannot be ruled out. Free flow of the tourists from East and Southeast Asia into the Northeast might make the region especially vulnerable to the problems of drugs, smuggling, HIV/AIDS, poaching and also labor migration. These are ground realities to which we cannot close our eyes. In anticipation of these probable dangers, do we close our doors or do we find ways and means to deal with them? Problems are there and will always be there. What we need to focus on is the fact that to keep up with the changing times and with the concept of globalization we will have to make practical choices.

Conclusion

There is no doubt that the Look East Policy is making an impressive headway but there is the danger that it may get delinked from the vision of the Northeast as a gateway. There has been some excitement about ASEAN-India Car Rally, inauguration of the Bangkok-Guwahati air-service (whose service has often been interrupted), international status of the Guwahati Airport, inauguration of the India built road in Myanmar and the proposal of the Home Ministry to reopen the Stilwell Road. There is no doubt that closer relations with Southeast Asia will open significant possibilities for the Northeast and the changing geography of global tourism might make opening of our eastern doors to tourists from the Asia-Pacific region a very attractive proposition. Giving a substantial thrust to the Look East Policy would require settling the numerous conflicts of the Northeast through a comprehensive approach. Moreover, it would be necessary to break free from the "security prism" and seek a general opening of the region in intellectual, cultural, political and economic arenas. Dreams do not turn into reality by themselves, the idea of transforming the Northeast into a Mecca for tourists will have to be the focus of a grand project involving the government, civil society plus corporate and multilateral actors. Projects will have to be specially designed and their social and environmental impact carefully assessed. This will require substantial investments not only in terms of money but investment of political and intellectual energy. These are serious challenges and choices that will have to be made for the Northeast to fulfill its potential.

REFERENCES

1. Kuppuswamy, C.S.: "India's Look East Policy: More aggressive, Better dividends", www.saag.org-paper No. 1663.
2. Baruah, Sanjib: "Of broken promises and false starts", http://www.telegraphindia.com/1050412/asp/opinion/story_4590622.asp
3. Speech delivered by Sanjoy Hazarika at the International Conference for Regional Cooperation, Margherita College, Assam, January 19, 2004.
4. Ministry of Tourism (Government of India) website.
5. *Figures 2005 Incredible India*: Ministry of Tourism, Government of India, New Delhi, August 2006.
6. *Ibid*.
7. "What is Ecotourism", http://www.ecotourism.org.au/
8. Honey, Martha: *Ecotourism and Sustainable Development — who owns paradise*?
9. Speech delivered by Sanjoy Hazarika: *op.cit*.
10. Baruah, Sanjib: *op.cit*.
11. *Ibid*.
12. *Ibid*.
13. Ramesh, Jairam: "Northeast India in a new Asia", http://www.india-seminar.com/2005/550/550%20jairam%20ramesh.htm
14. Rao, Nina, Suresh, K.T.: "Ecotourism and Sustainable development", http://www.equitabletourism.org/ecotourism.htm

Sources Cited

1. Barua, Sanjib – *The Problem*, http://www.manipuronline.com/North-East/November2005/theproblem23_2.htm
2. Ministry of DoNER website

13

VALEDICTORY ADDRESS

D.D. Lapang

Ladies and Gentlemen

It is an honor and a privilege to be associated with this seminar, a seminar having a very important theme "Look East Policy: Impact on Northeast India". The Look East Policy was initiated by the Union Government. This Policy carries a message which has a vision, mission and determination. The Government of India accepts the fact that the northeastern region is located in the farflung part of India, an area where backwardness and underdevelopment persist. On numerous occasions the Government of India has exercised its mind to bring the Northeast into the mainstream standard of living and to merge the region with the times. This region has been perceived by the Government of India as a younger sister of the other regions of the country. Shri H. D. Deve Gowda the then Prime Minister of India was moved when he visited the region and he announced a package of 6100 crores to be invested in the region. The package was declared but the ground realities did not materialize as expected. Initiating this policy the Government of India contends that the Northeast should not only be a corridor for the implementation of this policy vis-à-vis the Southeast Asian countries but that the region must extract the benefits of this policy. India needs to discover a better standard in its economy and welfare. The Look East Policy is a springboard for the region and the country to leap to a position higher than what they already are today. This seminar saw the involvement of dignitaries and participants from different professions. Participants put their heads, hearts and minds together towards the same goal to see a better tomorrow. The seminar was organized and conducted in a serious, thorough and the purposeful manner. The remarks observed at the seminar conveyed a down to earth message to the people of the Northeast. Those at the helm of affairs needed to exhibit the qualities of responsibility, credibility and accountability. The philosophy, the doctrine and the ideology of the Look East Policy call on India to engage with its neighbors, to open the golden gate for the outside world to enter India through key areas of its economy. God and nature have blessed this region with abundant potential. Exposure to the wider global atmosphere means pushing ourselves to a better horizon of hope and a better destiny for a brighter tomorrow and for the coming generations. The Look East Policy demands intensified diplomatic and economic ties with countries of Southeast Asia, a region which represents a ten member group of nations who demonstrate a rapid economic growth in the zonal strategic calculus. In 1995 India demonstrated its international importance when it was elevated to the level of a full dialogue partner of ASEAN. It participated in the forum where security concerns of ASEAN were discussed and addressed. India has traditionally been in partnership with the CLMV—Cambodia, Laos, Myanmar and Vietnam engaging with these countries through the Mekong-Ganga partnership. The Look East Policy has also included South Asian and Southeast Asian neighbors in BIMSTEC — Bay of Bengal Initiative for Multi-Sectoral Technical and Economic Cooperation. The member nations of this group are: Bangladesh, India, Myanmar, Sri Lanka, Thailand,

Bhutan and Nepal. These seven nations have approved a plan for a free trade pact by 2017 while the three most advanced countries in the region, India, Sri Lanka and Thailand, are committed to trade liberalization by 2012. It is India's desire to surge ahead through such economic partnerships in engaging with the outside world.

The Look East policy envisages the Northeast not as the periphery of India but as a centrally positioned area integrating two dynamic regions—mainland India and the Southeast Asian countries. To translate this policy into ground reality the Northeast region should be equipped with a vast and elaborate network so that highways, railways, telecommunications, transmission lines crisscross the whole region. The Northeast has great potential to promote tourism, agriculture, horticulture, fishery, hydroelectric power, oil and natural gas and human resource. The human resource of this region is abundantly blessed. The young boys and girls of this region speak proficient English and many have traveled to work in different cities in India and even abroad. The call centers at New Delhi have employed thousands of youth from this region. The question is, why should we simply send our younger generation to distant places to seek employment? This drain of human resource can be addressed if we make model, modern avenues within the region itself where their potential can be harnessed. We are back to the root of the problem as we lack infrastructure where we can accommodate these educated and talented young minds. Similarly the poor physical connectivity hinders the Northeast region from fully realizing the benefits of cross-border economic exchange. The Look East policy can have an immense economic impact for this region and it is important for us to capitalize on its potential. The need of the hour is to develop infrastructure and to invite investment and investors. However a lot of work needs to be done. Investors visiting this region have many questions to reassure their interest. First, the security aspect- are they safe to invest their money? Is the political climate conducive to investment? Will insurgency hamper their investment? These concerns will have to be minimized and subsequently eradicated for no person will invest his money if the climate is not safe. The second concern relates to the lack of infrastructure development in terms of roads, communication, marketability of the region's produce and also the support of the local people. Absence of these basic requirements will deny us the capability of marching with the times. To give a fillip to air connectivity the abandoned World War II airstrips which dot the Southeast Asian region can be made operational. Thus the blue-print to investment should ensure that all aspects of connectivity are included right from road connectivity to marketability of produce. The Stillwell road connecting Yunnan province in China upto Ledo in Assam through Myanmar needs to be improved and made functional. Other land routes should be opened to encourage pilgrimage and tourism. Procedures and formalities need to be simplified to facilitate better relations with neighbors to ensure that trade agreements entered into by the centre with neighboring countries and cross-border movements of goods and services are conveniently executed.

There are a number of hurdles and dislocations in realizing these objectives. The land tenure system in the Northeast stands in the way. Financial institutions are unable to come forward and invest money because land cannot be mortgaged. Another area of development that needs attention is the promotion of tourism. Tourism is the central focus of growth and can improve the economic condition of the people. Tourism offers immense employment opportunities because it supports allied sectors. If this sector cannot be improved there will be a serious dislocation in development. This region's pace will remain slow and it will not be able to avail all the facilities available in the market. Negotiations are being carried on by the Government of India for a free trade agreement with its neighbors. If this agreement is executed the meaning of Look East Policy will be put into place as it will address the ground realities. We should encourage the free movement of vehicles, goods and services from one part of the country to another. If barriers exist people will be restricted in their movements and will be unsuccessful in their initiatives. Today the Northeast has become a transit and trade can be carried on very meaningfully if provided with the right incentives.

The people of the Northeast have been demanding for all categories of development, development of roads, schools and so on. However there is one category of development which has not received adequate attention and that is the development of mankind. A person may have a beautiful palatial building, well decorated and architecturally admirable but to be complete its occupants must also possess the appropriate qualities. If the occupants of such a building are crooks, brutes, hoodlums, criminals and murderers then what will be the image of that building? If the occupants of such a structure do not know how to utilize its facilities then the structure's presentation is incomplete. Such a situation calls for the development of mankind. This requires the development of a positive attitude, mentality and lifestyle of people. This requires people to shed their cocoon mentality, to grow and march with the times. There is a wrong conception about keeping our identity by driving the 'other' away. The actual conception of identity is to preserve all that you have and take whatever opportunities are available in the market. Identity can be maintained anywhere irrespective of our place of residence. We have to change our mindset to these realities.

It is our desire to see that the region enjoys the maximum benefit that the Look East Policy has to offer. Many policies have been announced yet a number of them have failed to see the light of day. This should not be the case with the Look East Policy. It is our desire to see that the people of the Northeast are well off economically, socially and politically. We dream of a better India but it is also imperative that we dream of better Indians. The late Rajiv Gandhi echoed similar thoughts when he said "I have nurtured a dream, a dream of a new India where every Indian is a pride of everyone". If our children go anywhere they should exemplify the attributes of good Indians that the world will appreciate. We would like to see that every Indian is a child and pride of the country.

Thank you.

14

VOTE OF THANKS

Merostar Rani

The Chief Guest at this valedictory session of the Seminar, Dr. D.D. Lapang, Chairman of the Meghalaya Economic Development Council,

The Principal of Synod College, Dr. D. Wanswett, the Vice Principal Mrs. P.R. Lyngskor, resource persons, distinguished guests, and all present,

It is said that gratitude means paying the first installment of the debt and for the fruit of success that we have all tasted in the form of this National Seminar, I, on behalf of the organizing body, the Internal Quality Assurance Cell of the Synod College, stand here in all humility to express my gratitude to many kind and helpful individuals and organizations that have stretched out their helping hands towards making this seminar a great success and a memorable experience where the Look East Policy has been redefined.

The Chief Guest at the inauguration, Hon'ble Union Minister of State for Commerce, Shri Jairam Ramesh, deserves three cheers for his brilliant discourse on the policy and his deep concern for the growth and development of the Northeast India. We are indeed grateful to you Sir for inaugurating the seminar and for the keynote address. The Chief Minister of Meghalaya, Shri J. D. Rymbai, is specially thanked for chairing the inaugural function and for all the help and support rendered during the preparation of the seminar and for continuing to be a source of inspiration. I am grateful to Dr. Donkupar Roy, Deputy Chief Minister of Meghalaya, and, of course, our benefactor Shri P. A. Sangma who has always been our mentor and friend. I also thank Shri Rajiv Pratap Rudy, former Union Minister of State, Commerce and Civil Aviation (Independent Charge) and Prof. D.P. Tripathi, National General Secretary, Nationalist Congress Party for sparing their valuable time to be part of this seminar. I also express my gratitude to all the chairpersons, resource persons, invitees and participants who have traveled from far and near to be present in this seminar and to engage in its deliberations.

I also express my sincere appreciation and gratefulness to Dr. D.D. Lapang, Chairman, Meghalaya Economic Development Council for having accepted our invitation to attend the inaugural function and to grace today's valedictory function as the Chief Guest.

I also place on record my sincere thanks to the Principal of the college, Dr. D. Wanswett, members of the organizing committee, the Advisory committee, the IQAC, the teachers, the establishment staff, the students and in particular cadets of the Synod College NCC units and the members of the Synod College choir for their dedication and hard work in seeing that the various sessions of the seminar were conducted smoothly.

The sponsors have played a big role in enabling us to hold this seminar on such a grand scale. Thanks are due to the chief sponsors the North Eastern Council, Shillong and the patrons, the Tourism Department, Government of

Meghalaya under the leadership of the Tourism Minister, Shri R.G. Lyngdoh, India Tourism, Guwahati and AIRCEL, Shillong.

Finally a note of appreciation to the Deputy Commissioner, East Khasi Hills, the Public Works Department, Government of Meghalaya, the Directorate of Information and Public Relations, Government of Meghalaya, the Shillong Municipal Board, the Meghalaya Police and the print and electronic media, who all have contributed valuable assistance to the seminar. I thank them all once again and thank each and every one present at this valedictory function.

INDEX

K

L

M

N

■■■